English Grammar for Students of Russian

**The Study Guide
for Those Learning Russian**

Second edition

D0074568

*Edwina J. Cruise
Mount Holyoke College*

The Olivia and Hill Press®

ENGLISH GRAMMAR series

English Grammar for Students of French
English Grammar for Students of Spanish
English Grammar for Students of German
English Grammar for Students of Italian
English Grammar for Students of Latin
English Grammar for Students of Japanese
Gramática española para estudiantes de inglés

Printed in the U.S.A.

Library of Congress Catalog Card Number: 87-7889

ISBN 0-934034-21-4

CONTENTS

PREFACE

English Grammar for Students of Russian explains basic terminology and concepts of English grammar, focusing on material which will most benefit students of Russian. It is written for native speakers of English, but assumes no formal knowledge of English grammar; therefore it is written in very simple language.

This handbook is designed to supplement any beginning Russian language textbook. Each short chapter is a self-contained discussion of a particular grammar topic. A brief definition is followed by an explanation, with examples, of the way the grammatical construction is used in English. Then a parallel section illustrates the use of the same grammar point in Russian, step by step, using sample sentences translated from English into Russian. In some chapters, structures that are likely to cause problems for the student of Russian are singled out for special attention. Extensive cross-references and an index make it possible to locate information quickly.

This book is not meant to be comprehensive, nor is it intended to replace a language textbook. Although it includes most of the topics presented in an elementary language textbook, exceptions to Russian grammatical rules have been omitted, along with points which have no English equivalents.

Thanks to grants from the International Research and Exchanges Board (IREX), I have participated in two Summer Exchanges of Language Teachers at Moscow State University. I am pleased to acknowledge my gratitude to the superb instructors of that program and to IREX. Special thanks to my students at Mount Holyoke College; their enthusiasm for the Russian language motivated me to write this book. They will understand why so many examples use the word horse.

EJC, 1987

For the second edition short reviews have been added at the end of most chapters. If you have learned the material, you should not have any problems with these exercises. After you have completed them, compare your answers with the Answer Key at the end of the handbook. If they don't match, use your mistakes as a guide to locate in the chapter what you have not mastered.

EJC, 1993

INTRODUCTION

Learning a foreign language, in this case Russian, requires that you look at a word in three ways:

1. The **meaning** of the word. An English word must be connected to a Russian word that has an equivalent meaning. For example, the English word *horse* has the same meaning as the Russian word **ло́шадь**.

   You learn new vocabulary in Russian by memorizing each new word and its English equivalent. Memorizing vocabulary is a time consuming, but essential part of learning a foreign language. Here are a few tips to help you remember the meanings of Russian words.

   Many times knowing one Russian word will help you learn another; Russian has many **cognates,** that is, words related to each other because they are based on a common stem or root.

   The verb **писа́ть**, *to write*, for example, with its root **пис-**, is connected to

писа́тель	*writer*
письмо́	*letter*
описа́ние	*description*
переписа́ть	*to rewrite*

   and many other words which share the same root. If you take the time to study common Russian roots (which your textbook and your teacher will point out) you will find it easier to remember vocabulary.

   Sometimes words with the same or related meanings are similar in English and Russian. Russian has borrowed many words from English; these borrowed or **loan words** are especially prevalent in sports, transport and technology.

English	**Russian**
radio	ра́дио
television	телеви́зор
transport	тра́нспорт
volleyball	волейбо́л
bus	авто́бус

2. The **class** of the word. Words are grouped by types, each type being a **part of speech**. Depending on its part of speech, a word will

follow certain rules. You must be able to identify what part of speech a word belongs to so that you will know what rules to apply.

In this handbook we will discuss seven different parts of speech.

noun	verb
pronoun	adverb
adjective	preposition
	conjunction

Look at the word *love* in the following sentences.

I *love* speaking Russian.
   verb

My *love* is like a beach ball: round.
    noun

He is famous for writing *love* stories.
      adjective

In English the word "love" looks the same in all three sentences, but each "love" belongs to a different part of speech. To translate these three meanings of *love* into Russian we would need to use three different words, each following a different set of rules. This handbook will help you to recognize parts of speech so that you can choose the correct Russian equivalent and know which rules apply.

3. The **use** of the word. In addition to its class as a part of speech, a word must be defined according to the role it plays in the sentence. Each word, whether English or Russian, serves a unique function within the sentence. Determining the function of a word will help you to use it properly in English and will help you to find the proper Russian equivalent.

Look at the word *her* in the following sentences.

All the students admire *her*.
      direct object

The teacher gave *her* an "A."
     indirect object

Are you going to graduate with *her?*
    object of preposition *with*

In English the word for "her" looks the same in all three sentences, but in Russian the word will be different in each instance because it has a different use in each sentence.

As a student of Russian you must pay special attention to the relationship of words within a sentence. Look at the differences between the two sentences below. Note the changes that occur as the subject of the sentence changes from *woman* to *man.*

> *This is that young* **woman** *who was reading.*
> Это **та** молод**а́я же́нщина**, кото́**рая** чита́**ла**.

> *This is that young* **man** *who was reading.*
> Это **тот** молод**о́й челове́к**, кото́**рый** чита́**л**.

In the English sentence we have changed one word, *woman,* to *man.* This change does not affect any other word in the sentence. In the Russian sentence, by contrast, the substitution of the word *man* for *woman* affects the endings for *that, young, who* and *was reading.*

For most English speakers, studying Russian presents a special challenge: we must be able to understand the precise grammatical relationship of words to each other so that we can select the correct form of each word to express that relationship.

1. WHAT IS A NOUN?

A **noun** is a word that names:

- a person   husband, clown, girl,
                    Professor Jones, Mark, Bonnie
- an animal   dog, bird, bear, horse
                    Rover, Blackie, Grendel
- a place   city, state, country, continent
                    South Hadley, USA, Moscow, Russia
- a thing   vodka, saddle, dresser,
                    Moscow River, Cosmos Hotel
- an event   marriage, death, football
                    robbery, rest, growth
- an idea   poverty, racism, humor, mathematics
  or quality   strength, elegance, virtue, grace

As you can see, a noun can name something tangible, i.e., that you can touch *(dog, flower, skin, White House)* or it can name something abstract, i.e., that you can't physically touch but you can grasp with your mind *(love, patience, literature)*.

IN ENGLISH
A noun that always begins with a capital letter, such as the name of a person or a place *(Professor Jones, Moscow)*, is called a **proper noun**. A noun that does not begin with a capital letter, except when it starts a sentence *(university, milk, car),* is called a **common noun**.

A noun that names a collection or group of things or people *(furniture, army, family)* is called a **collective noun**.

A noun that is made up of two words is called a **compound noun**. A compound noun can be a common noun, such as *comic strip* and *ice cream,* or a proper noun such as *Red Square* and *North America.*

Sometimes words may look like nouns, but function as adjectives (see **What is an Adjective?**, p. 60).

Noun	Adjective
a room	at *room* temperature
a street	a *street* fair
Moscow	*Moscow* water

To help you recognize nouns, here is a paragraph where the nouns are in italics.

> ...And leaving the *question* unanswered she fell to reading the *sign-boards*. "*Office* and *warehouse*... Dental *surgeon*... Yes, I will tell *Dolly everything*. She doesn't like *Vronsky*... *Fillipov, rolls*—I've heard he sells his *pastry* to *Petersburg*. The Moscow[1] *water* is so good. Ah, the *springs* at *Mitishchen*, and the *pancakes*!..." And she remembered how long ago, when she was a *girl* of seventeen, she had gone with her *aunt* to visit the Troitsa[1] *Monastery*.

(Lev Tolstoy, *Anna Karenina*)

Terms Used to Talk About Nouns

GENDER—A noun has gender, which we classify as masculine, feminine, or neuter (see **What is Meant by Gender?**, p. 7).

NUMBER—A noun has number, which we identify as singular or plural (see **What is Meant by Number?**, p. 10).

FUNCTION—A noun can have a variety of functions. We can recognize the function of a noun by its position in the sentence or by the way it ends, which is called case (see **What is Meant by Case?**, p. 14).

IN RUSSIAN
Nouns generally have the same function as in English.

---

[1]This is an example of a noun used as an adjective, that is, to describe another noun (see **What is an Adjective?**, p. 60).

▼▼▼▼▼▼▼▼▼▼▼▼▼▼REVIEW ▼▼▼▼▼▼▼▼▼▼▼▼▼▼▼▼▼

Underline the nouns in the sentences below.

1. The Jones went on a tour to the seashore.

2. Moscow, the capital of Russia, is a city rich in culture.

3. Reading is a very popular pastime on Russian subways.

4. Patience is an underrated virtue.

5. Many Russians regard Pushkin as the father of their literary heritage.

6. The students all displayed diligence and perseverance.

7. The former Soviet Union suffers from a high rate of alcoholism.

8. The price of food increases, but my salary remains the same.

2. WHAT IS MEANT BY GENDER?

Gender is the grammatical classification of a word as masculine, feminine, or neuter. Gender plays a much less visible role in English than in Russian.

IN ENGLISH

Grammatical gender is very often the same as natural gender, which is the classification of a noun according to the sex of the being which the noun defines.

In other words, gender in English normally reflects the noun's biological sex: male beings are masculine, female beings are feminine. Objects and abstract ideas are neuter. When we use a noun we may not realize that it has gender. But when we replace the noun with *he, she*, or *it*, we choose one of these three words without hesitation because we automatically give a gender to the noun we are replacing.

A noun is of the **masculine gender** if *he* or *him* is used to substitute for the noun.

> The *boy* came home; *he* was tired, and I was glad to see *him*.

A noun is of the **feminine gender** if *she* or *her* is used to substitute for the noun.

> My *aunt* came for a visit; *she* is nice and I like *her*.

A noun is of the **neuter gender** if *it* is used to substitute for the noun.

> There is a *tree* in front of the house. *It* is a maple.

IN RUSSIAN

A noun is either masculine, feminine, or neuter, depending on how the word ends. You can almost always tell the gender of a noun from its ending in the dictionary.

A noun is masculine if it ends in a consonant not followed by a soft sign (ь):

дом	*house*
брат	*brother*
май	*May*

A noun is feminine if it ends in an **-а** or **-я**:

кни́га	*book*
му́зыка	*music*
тётя	*aunt*

A noun is neuter if it ends in an **-o** or **-e**:

письмо́	*letter*
окно́	*window*
упражне́ние	*exercise*

Careful

There are several exceptions to these basic rules. Among them are two important categories:

1. Some natural gender nouns which define male persons and include the familiar forms of male names end in **-a**:

дя́дя	*uncle*
па́па	*daddy*
мужчи́на	*man*
Ва́ня	*Vanya*

2. Nouns which end in a soft sign (**ь**) may be masculine or feminine. There are several rules which can help you to determine the gender of this type of noun, but for now, you should plan to memorize gender as you learn the meaning of the word.

дочь	feminine	*daughter*
слова́рь	masculine	*dictionary*
го́лубь	masculine	*dove*
мышь	feminine	*mouse*

Just as in English, the pronoun you use to replace a noun depends on the gender of the noun (see **What is a Personal Pronoun?,** p. 36).

▼▼▼▼▼▼▼▼▼▼▼▼▼▼REVIEW ▼▼▼▼▼▼▼▼▼▼▼▼▼▼

You can almost always determine the gender of most Russian nouns without using a dictionary. Circle the appropriate letter: (M) masculine, (F) feminine, (N) neuter or (?) next to a noun whose gender you would need to look up.

1. журна́л	M	F	N	?
2. соба́ка	M	F	N	?
3. дождь	M	F	N	?
4. у́хо	M	F	N	?
5. молоко́	M	F	N	?
6. семья́	M	F	N	?
7. зда́ние	M	F	N	?
8. бык	M	F	N	?
9. ло́шадь	M	F	N	?
10. музе́й	M	F	N	?

3. WHAT IS MEANT BY NUMBER?

Number describes whether a word is singular or plural. When a word refers to one person or thing, it is said to be **singular** ; when it refers to more than one, it is called **plural** . Some nouns are used only in the singular or only in the plural, i.e., *darkness* (singular noun), *pants* (plural noun).

A plural noun is usually spelled differently and sounds different from the singular.

IN ENGLISH

We indicate the plural of nouns in several ways:

- most commonly by adding **-s** or **-es** to a singular noun

book	$\rightarrow$	book**s**
kiss	$\rightarrow$	kiss**es**

- sometimes by making a more significant change

man	$\rightarrow$	men
leaf	$\rightarrow$	leaves
child	$\rightarrow$	children
mouse	$\rightarrow$	mice

Nouns used only in the singular include: collective nouns that refer to an entire group of persons or things, and abstract nouns, which refer to a quality or an idea.

The *family* is leaving for Chicago today.
Sleep is my cat's favorite pastime.

IN RUSSIAN

A singular noun is made plural by adding or changing an ending. Although there are important exceptions, you can usually predict the plural of a noun if you know its singular.

Sometimes the stress, that is, where you put the emphasis when you pronounce the word, changes from singular to plural.

- Most masculine nouns and all feminine nouns take **-ы** or **-и** in the plural.

кни́га	кни́ги	*book*	*books*
журнали́ст	журнали́ст**ы**	*journalist*	*journalists*

- All neuter nouns and some masculine nouns take **-a** or **-я** in the plural.

окно́	о́кна	*window*	*windows*
дом	дома́	*house*	*houses*

Some nouns exist only in the singular or only in the plural.

- Nouns used only in the singular include collective and abstract nouns.

ме́бель	*furniture*
любо́вь	*love*
лук	*onion(s)*

- Some nouns are used only in the plural.

штаны́	*pants*
но́жницы	*scissors*
де́ньги	*money*
щи	*cabbage soup*

▼▼▼▼▼▼▼▼▼▼▼▼▼▼▼▼▼▼▼▼REVIEW ▼▼▼▼▼▼▼▼▼▼▼▼▼▼▼▼▼▼▼

I. Here is a list of English nouns in the plural. Write the singular form of each noun.

1. dresses _____

2. loaves _____

3. families _____

4. teeth _____

5. women _____

II. Here is a list of Russian nouns in their singular and plural forms.
- Under the PLURAL column, circle the part of the word that indicates a plural form.

Singular	Plural
1. университе́т	университе́ты
2. рука́	ру́ки
3. мо́ре	моря́
4. дверь	две́ри
5. час	часы́
6. музе́й	музе́и
7. лицо́	ли́ца
8. дом	дома́

4. WHAT ARE INDEFINITE AND DEFINITE ARTICLES?

An **article** is a word which is placed before a noun to show if the noun refers to a particular person, place, thing, animal, or idea, or if the noun refers to an unspecified person, place, thing, animal or idea.[1]

IN ENGLISH

The indefinite article **a** or **an** is placed before a singular noun to show that a noun does not refer to a specific person, place, thing, animal or idea.

▪ use *a* before a word beginning with a consonant

I saw *a* militiaman on Pushkin Street.
not a specific militiaman

▪ use *an* before a word beginning with a vowel

I ate *an* orange.
not a specific orange.

Plural nouns that do not refer back to something or someone specific are used without an article.

Chekhov wrote stories.
unspecified stories

The definite article *the* is placed before a singular or plural noun if it refers to a specific person, place, thing, animal or idea.

I saw *the* militiaman on Pushkin Street.
a specific militiaman

I ate *the* oranges.
specific oranges

---

[1]Since the article modifies a noun, it is considered an adjective (see **What is an Adjective?**, p. 60).

IN RUSSIAN

There are no articles. When a sentence is translated into English, articles, if appropriate, must be added. Your knowledge of English and the meaning of the sentence will help you to add the article *(a, an* or *the)* which best suits the meaning of the sentence or paragraph.

Что э́то? Это кни́га.
*What is this? This is **a** book.*

Где кни́га? На столе́.
*Where is **the** book? On **the** table.*

Even though there are no articles in Russian, we need to be aware of their use in English. The form of the noun in Russian may depend upon whether or not the noun refers to someone or something in particular, identified by the definite article in English, or to someone or something unspecified, identified by the indefinite article.

*I didn't buy **the books**.*
        the definite article
        refers to specific books
Я не купи́л **кни́ги**.
        the accusative case (see p. 16)
        expresses a specific object

*I didn't buy **books**.*
        absence of an article
        there is no specific object
Я не купи́л **книг**.
        the genitive case (see p. 16)
        expresses negation when the object is not specific

5. WHAT IS MEANT BY CASE?

Case is the form of a word which shows how that word functions within the sentence.

IN ENGLISH

The order of words in a sentence helps us to recognize the function of the nouns and shows us the meaning of the whole sentence. We easily recognize the difference in meaning between the following two sentences purely on the basis of word order. The nouns themselves do not change even though they serve a different function in each sentence.

> The girl baked Mother a cake.
>> The *girl* is baking the cake and *Mother* is receiving it.
>
> Mother baked the girl a cake.
>> *Mother* is baking the cake and the *girl* is receiving it.

The words *girl* and *Mother* do not change form, no matter what function they perform in the sentence. It is word order that shows us the meaning of the sentence.

In English there are only a few instances in which we can see changes in the spelling or endings of a word as the word assumes a new function in the sentence.

We are most aware of case in English when we use pronouns (see **What is a Pronoun?**, p. 33). Pronouns can help us to recognize different cases in English. In the two sentences below, it is not just word order, but also the form, i.e., the case, of the pronoun which affects the meaning of the sentence.

> I know *them.*
> They know *me.*

We cannot say "I know *they,*" or "They know *I,*" because the forms *they* and *I* cannot be used as objects of a verb (see **What are Objects?**, p. 24). Let us study case in English in more detail by looking at pronouns. If you can recognize the different cases in English, you will find it much easier to understand the more extensive use of case in Russian.

English pronouns have three cases.

The **subjective case** → for subjects and predicate words (see **What is a Subject?**, p. 19 and **What is a Predicate?**, p. 30).

He and *I* went to the Kremlin yesterday.

subjects → subjective case

We looked at Ivan the Terrible's bell tower.

subject →subjective case

I never heard of Ivan the Terrible. *Who* is *he?*

subject→   subject→   predicate→
subjective case   subjective case subjective case

The **objective case** → for direct objects, indirect objects and objects of prepositions (see **What are Objects?**, p. 24 and **What is a Preposition?**, p. 93).

They invited *him* and *me* to the Bolshoi Theater.

subject →   direct objects →
subjective case objective case

After the play, *they* made *us* a wonderful dinner.

              subject →   indirect object →
              subjective case objective case

subject →   subject→
subjective case   subjective case

We asked about *her* when *we* saw *them.*

              object of preposition→ direct object→
              objective case   objective case

In these examples pronouns have different forms depending on how they are used in the sentence. The different cases prevent us from saying "*Us* went to the theater" or "*Him* talked about *she.*"

The **possessive case** → to show ownership. The possessive pronoun can function as subject, predicate, direct object, indirect object or object of the preposition.

This book is Sacha's. *Yours* is on the table.

              possessive pronoun → subject

This book about Tolstoy is *yours.*

              possessive pronoun → predicate

I like your friends, but I love *mine.*

              possessive pronoun → direct object

Misha called his friends, but I wrote *mine* a letter.
possessive pronoun → indirect object

Vika studied for her test, but Dima didn't study for *his*.
possessive pronoun → object of preposition

The possessive case is discussed in a separate section, **What is a Possessive Pronoun?**, p. 44.

IN RUSSIAN
Word order alone rarely identifies the function of any word in a sentence. Usually its role is indicated by the way in which the word ends, otherwise referred to as the **case ending**. The different endings that a Russian word may have correspond to its several possible functions in a sentence.

All the possible forms for any word that changes case are called a **declension**. When you have memorized all the case endings that a word can have, you are then able to "decline" that word.

There are three basic types of words or parts of speech which decline: nouns, pronouns and adjectives (see **What is a Noun?**, p. 4; **What is a Pronoun?**, p. 33; and **What is an Adjective?**, p. 60). There are different declension patterns for each part of speech and some variations within the same part of speech.

There are six cases in Russian. Although the order of case endings given in Russian language textbooks varies, the following sequence is common.

1. The **nominative case** → for the subject of the sentence and for many predicate words in the sentence. (See **What is a Subject?**, p. 19, and **What is a Predicate?**, p. 30.)

2. The **genitive case** → to show possession and for objects of some prepositions. (See **What is the Possessive?**, p. 22 and **What is a Preposition?**, p. 93.)

3. The **dative case** → for indirect objects and for objects of some prepositions. (See **What are Objects?**, p. 24 and **What is a Preposition?**, p. 93.)

4. The **accusative case** → for direct objects and for objects of some prepositions. (See **What are Objects?**, p. 24 and **What is a Preposition?**, p. 93.)

5. The **instrumental case** → expresses the means, manner, or agent by which an action is performed. It is also used for objects of some prepositions and in some instances for objects which require the use of a predicate word. (See **What is a Predicate?**, p. 30 and **What is a Preposition?**, p. 93.)

6. The **prepositional case**, sometimes called the **locative case** → commonly used in phrases preceded by prepositions which define a space or location. It is the only case which is always used with a preposition. Many, but not all, prepositions take objects in the prepositional case. (See **What is a Preposition?**, p. 93).

Let us see how declension works in Russian by looking at the word **газéта** *(newspaper),* a feminine noun, in all its cases. Although case endings may differ for nouns of different gender, the principle is the same for all nouns.

A noun is always listed in the dictionary or in the vocabulary section of your textbook in the nominative case.

> газéта   *newspaper*

To form the other cases, remove the nominative case ending, if there is one, and add the ending given in your textbook.

Case	Singular	Plural
nominative	газéт-**а**	газéт-**ы**
genitive	газéт-**ы**	газéт-
dative	газéт-**е**	газéт-**ам**
accusative	газéт-**у**	газéт-**ы**
instrumental	газéт-**ой**	газéт-**ами**
prepositional	газéт-**е**	газéт-**ах**

Now let us see how the word **газéта** changes its case ending as it assumes different functions in the three sentences below.

The newspaper is on the table.
Газéта на столé.

> *Newspaper* is the subject of the sentence; therefore we use the nominative case, **газéта**.

*I read about the fire **in the newspaper**.*
Я читáла о пожáре в **газéте**.

> *Newspaper* is the object of the preposition *in*, which here takes the prepositional case; therefore we use the prepositional case, **газéте**, after the preposition.

*Have you read today's **newspaper**?*
Вы читáли сегóдняшнюю **газéту**?

> *Newspaper* is the direct object of the verb; therefore we use
> the accusative case, **газéту**.

As you can see in the sentences above, you must determine how a noun functions in a sentence before you can choose the correct form of the word. Here are steps that you should follow.

The boy gave the girl the newspapers.

1. GENDER—Identify the gender and number of each noun.

> boy → **мáльчик** is masculine singular.
> girl → **дéвушка** is feminine singular.
> newspapers → **газéты** is feminine plural.

2. FUNCTION—Determine how each noun functions in the sentence.

> boy → subject
> girl → indirect object
> newspapers → direct object

3. CASE—Determine what case in Russian corresponds to the function you have identified in step 2.

> boy → subject → nominative case
> girl → indirect object → dative case
> newspapers → direct object → accusative case

4. SELECTION—Choose the proper case ending for each of the nouns from the endings you have memorized.

> *The boy gave the girl the newspapers.*
> Мáльчик дал дéвушке газéты.

the boy	gave	the girl	the newspapers
nominative		dative	accusative
masc.		fem.	fem.
sing.		sing.	pl.

6. WHAT IS A SUBJECT?

The **subject** of a sentence is the person or thing that performs the action of the verb (see **What is a Verb?**, p. 68).

IN ENGLISH
When you wish to find the subject of a sentence, always look for the verb first; then ask *who?* or *what?* before the verb. The answer will be the subject.

> The landowner talks to the serf.
>> *Who* talks to the serf? Answer: the landowner.
>> *Landowner* is the singular subject.

> The children of the Count are at the door.
>> *Who* is at the door? Answer: the children.
>> *Children* is the plural subject.

> The tears rolled slowly down Princess Mary's face.
>> *What* rolled? Answer: the tears.
>> *Tears* is the plural subject.

Never assume that a word is the subject simply because it comes first in the sentence. A subject need not be first in the sentence, as you can see in the following examples in which the subjects are in **boldface** and the verbs are *italicized*.

> With eager haste the **Rostovs** *began* the hunt.
> Barking to her master, **Milka** *jumped up* in anticipation.

Some sentences have more than one subject and verb; you must be able to find the subject of each verb.

> The **author** *wrote* that all happy **families** *were* alike.
>> *Author* is the singular subject of *wrote,* and *families* is the plural subject of *were.*

In English and in Russian it is very important to find the subject of each verb and to make sure that the subject and the verb agree. You must choose the form of the verb which agrees with the subject: if the subject is singular, the verb must be singular; if the subject is plural, the verb must be plural. (See **What is a Verb Conjugation?**, p. 72.)

IN RUSSIAN

As a rule the subject behaves the same way in Russian as it does in English. It answers the one-word question **кто?** *(who?)* or **что?** *(what?)* asked before the verb. The subject of a Russian sentence is normally in the nominative case (see **What is Meant by Case?**, p. 14).

*The **professor** is reading slowly.*
Профéссор читáет мéдленно.

              verb 3rd pers. sing.

subject → nominative
masc. sing.

*The **letter** was lying over there.*
Письмó лежáло там.

           verb 3rd pers. sing.

subject → nominative
neut. sing.

*Does **Anna** speak Russian?*
Áнна говорит по-рýсски?

         verb 3rd pers. sing.

subject → nominative
fem. sing.

*How well **we** live!*
Как хорошó **мы** живём!

                verb 1st pers. pl.

          subject → nominative
          pl.

▼▼▼▼▼▼▼▼▼▼▼▼▼▼▼REVIEW ▼▼▼▼▼▼▼▼▼▼▼▼▼▼▼▼▼▼

Find the subjects in the following sentences.
- Next to Q, write the question you need to ask to find the subject.
- Next to A, write the answer to the question you just asked.

1. When the bell rang, the children ran out.

Q:_____

A: _____

Q:_____

A: _____

2. One waiter took the order, another brought the food.

Q:_____

A: _____

Q:_____

A: _____

3. The first-year students voted for the class president.

Q:_____

A: _____

4. That assumes I am always right.

Q:_____

A: _____

Q:_____

A: _____

5. Difficult as it is, Russian is a beautiful language.

Q:_____

A: _____

Q:_____

A: _____

7. WHAT IS THE POSSESSIVE?

The term **possessive** means that one noun *owns* or *possesses* another noun.

Sasha has Tanya's book.
  possessor possessed

Natasha reads Pushkin's poetry.
  possessor   possessed

IN ENGLISH
You can show possession in one of two ways:

1. with an *apostrophe*

  ▪ by adding an apostrophe + **s** to a singular possessor noun or to a plural noun not ending in "s"

    Pushkin's poetry
    singular possessor

    the women's room
    plural possessor

  ▪ by adding an apostrophe to the plural possessor noun ending in "s"

    the girls' father
    the students' demonstration

2. with the word *of*

    the poetry *of* Pushkin
    the father *of* the girls

IN RUSSIAN
Possession is shown by using the genitive case for the possessor, in other words, for the noun that "owns" the other noun. The noun possessed goes into whatever case corresponds to its function in the sentence. The noun being possessed usually stands first in normal word order, but endings make clear the relationship of the two nouns. The genitive case answers the questions **кого́**? *(of whom?)*, **чего́**? *(of what?)* and **чей**? *(whose?)*.

The teacher's *book is on the table.*
Кни́га **учи́теля** на столе́.

        possessor → genitive sing.

noun possessed → nominative

*Tanya was reading the verses **of Pushkin.***
Та́ня чита́ла стихи́ **Пу́шкина.**

        possessor → genitive sing.

   noun possessed → accusative

*He is living in **our friends'** house.*
Он живёт в до́ме **на́ших друзе́й.**

        possessor → genitive pl.

   noun possessed → prepositional

There is no separate word in Russian for the word "of" in the sense of possession. **Дом друзе́й** means *the friends' house* or *the house of the friends*; either translation is correct.

Not every use of the genitive case in Russian expresses possession. Consult your textbook for other uses of the genitive case.

▼▼▼▼▼▼▼▼▼▼▼▼▼▼▼REVIEW ▼▼▼▼▼▼▼▼▼▼▼▼▼▼▼▼

The following are possessive constructions using the apostrophe.
- Write the alternate English structure using the word *of*.
- Underline the possessor in your new construction.

1. the cat's meow

_____

2. the books' cost

_____

3. my older sister's husband

_____

4. Whose letter? Nina's.

_____

5. Peter's second child.

_____

8. WHAT ARE OBJECTS ?

Objects are nouns or pronouns that receive the action of verbs or complete prepositional phrases.

Most sentences consist, at the very least, of a *subject* and a *verb*.

Students study.
subject   verb

The subject of a sentence is a *noun* or a *pronoun* (see **What is a Noun?**, p. 4 and **What is a Pronoun?**, p. 33). Most sentences, however, contain other nouns and pronouns. Many of these words function as objects. Objects are divided into three categories, depending on how they are used in a sentence. The three types of objects are: direct objects, indirect objects, and objects of a preposition (see **What is a Preposition?**, p. 93).

Direct Object

IN ENGLISH
The **direct object** receives the action of the verb directly, without prepositions separating the verb from the receiver. It answers the one-word question *whom?* or *what?* asked after the verb.

Pierre hugged the bear.
Pierre hugged *whom?* Answer: The bear.
Bear is the direct object.

Oblomov loves his bed.
Oblomov loves *what?* Answer: His bed.
Bed is the direct object.

IN RUSSIAN
The direct object behaves the same way as it does in English. It answers the one-word question **кого**? *(whom)* or **что**? *(what)* asked after the verb. The direct object is expressed by the accusative case.

*Alexei loved the **peasant girl**.*
Alexei loved *whom?* Answer: The peasant-girl.
Peasant-girl is the direct object in the accusative case.
Алексей любил **крестьянку**.

*Ivan drinks the **vodka**.*
>   Ivan drinks *what?* Answer: The vodka.
>   *Vodka* is the direct object in the accusative case.

Ивáн пьёт **вóдку.**

Indirect Object

IN ENGLISH

The **indirect object** also receives the action of the verb, but as its name implies, it differs from the direct object by receiving the action indirectly. The indirect object answers the two-word question *to whom?* or *for whom?* or *to what?* or *for what?* asked after the verb.

>   Tatiana wrote Onegin a letter.
>>   Tatiana wrote *to whom?* Answer: Onegin.
>>   *Onegin* is the indirect object.

>   She prepares her friends supper.
>>   She prepared *for whom?* Answer: Her friends.
>>   *Friends* is the indirect object.

In the two examples above the words "to" or "for" do not appear. We can rewrite these sentences inserting *to* and *for* without changing their meaning.

>   Tatiana wrote a letter *to* Onegin.
>   She prepared supper *for* her friends.

As the sentences above illustrate, the indirect object can be expressed in two different ways:

- with the indirect object before the direct object

>   Tatiana wrote Onegin a letter.
>   indirect   direct
>   object   object

In sentences of this type, where *to* or *for* is not included, the indirect object always comes after the verb, but before the direct object.

- with the indirect object after the direct object as part of a prepositional phrase starting with the preposition *to* or *for* (see below):

>   prepositional phrase
>   Tatiana wrote a letter to Onegin.
>   direct   indirect
>   object   object

In sentences of this type, when the indirect object comes after the direct object, the preposition *to* or *for* will always be included.

Careful

Not every use of *to* or *for* identifies an indirect object. *To* and *for* can also introduce other types of prepositional phrases (see **What is a Preposition?**, p. 93).

In sentences which do not contain a direct object the indirect object may be written with or without the *to* or *for.*

> Tatiana wrote Onegin.
> Tatiana wrote to Onegin.

Not all sentences contain objects. Never assume the presence of an object; always ask the appropriate questions first.

> The women work well.
>> The women work *whom* or *what?* No answer possible.
>> The women work *to* or *for whom?* or *to* or *for what?* No answer possible.

The sentence above has no objects. *Well* is an adverb telling how the women worked (see **What is an Adverb?,** p. 99).

IN RUSSIAN

As in English, the indirect object answers the question **комý**? *(to or for whom)* **чемý**? *(to or for what)*. The indirect object is expressed by the dative case.

> *She prepares supper **for friends**.*
>> She prepares supper *for whom?* Answer: For friends.
>> *Friends* is the indirect object in the dative case.
>
> Онá готóвит **друзья́м** у́жин.
> |
>   dative

> *I am writing a letter **to my mother**.*
>> I am writing a letter *to whom?* Answer: To (my) mother.
>> *Mother* is the indirect object in the dative case.
>
> Я пишý письмó **мáтери.**
> |
>   dative

When a sentence has both a direct object and an indirect object their order is not fixed. Case endings enable us to distinguish the direct object from the indirect object.

*I found **the book for Ivan**.*
Я нашла́ Ива́ну кни́гу.

                                  direct object → accusative
                                  fem. sing. noun

        indirect object → dative
        masc. sing. noun

*We gave **the books to Maria**.*
Мы да́ли кни́ги Мари́и.

                                  indirect object → dative
                                  fem. sing. noun

        direct object → accusative
        fem. pl. noun

In the two sentences above both objects end in the same letter, but the endings refer to different cases of words of different genders. It is very important to memorize the gender of nouns and the case endings so that you can correctly distinguish one object from another.

Object of a Preposition

IN ENGLISH

The noun or pronoun which follows the preposition (see **What is a Preposition?**, p. 93) is called the **object of the preposition.** The object of the preposition answers the two-word question made up of the preposition + *what?* or *whom?*

The tree is in the forest.

> The tree is *in what?* Answer: In the forest.
> *Forest* is the object of the preposition *in.*

Dobchinsky is walking with Bobchinsky.

> Dobchinsky is walking *with whom?* Answer: With Bobchinsky.
> *Bobchinsky* is the object of the preposition *with.*

IN RUSSIAN

The object of a preposition is as easy to identify as it is in English. Russian prepositions, however, have objects in several different cases: genitive, accusative, dative, instrumental, and, of course, the prepositional case, which is the only case always preceded by a preposition. As you memorize a preposition, you will need to learn the case (or cases) in which its objects are expressed.

To show you the variety of cases possible after a preposition, here are five different prepositions, each requiring a different case:

для э́того челове́ка   *for* this person

       genitive case after **для**

курс **по** Ахма́товой   a course *on* Akhmatova

       dative case after **по**

че́рез парк   *through* the park

accusative case after **че́рез**

пе́ред до́мом   *in front of* the house

instrumental case after **пе́ред**

о мои́х лошадя́х   *about* my horses

prepositional case after **о**

Careful

As a student of Russian you must watch out for the following pitfalls: some verbs that in English are followed by a prepositional phrase (a preposition and an object of the preposition) may have Russian equivalents without a preposition.

> *She is looking **for the book.***
>   She is looking *for what?* Answer: The book.
>   *The book* is the object of the preposition *for.*
> Она́ и́щет **кни́гу**.
>   accusative case
>   The verb **иска́ть** *(to look for)* here takes a direct object.

> *I am interested **in sports.***
>   I am interested *in what?* Answer: Sports.
>   *Sports* is the object of the preposition *in.*
> Я интересу́юсь **спо́ртом**.
>   instrumental case
>   The verb **интересова́ться** *(to be interested in)* takes the instrumental case.

*Listen **to me**!*
> Listen *to whom?* Answer: Me.
> *Me* is the indirect object, expressed here as the object of
> the preposition *to*.

Слу́шайте **меня́**!
> |
>   accusative case

The verb **слу́шать** (*to listen to*) takes a direct object.

When you memorize Russian verbs do not automatically assume that they will behave in the same way as their English equivalents. Study carefully the case of the object that follows them.

▼▼▼▼▼▼▼▼▼▼▼▼▼▼▼**REVIEW** ▼▼▼▼▼▼▼▼▼▼▼▼▼▼▼▼

Below are sentences with direct and indirect objects.
- Circle the direct objects.
- Underline the indirect objects.

1. I baked mother a cake.

2. Throw mama from the train a kiss.

3. I picked flowers for Vika.

4. I drank mother's tea.

5. Mother, give me a kiss.

9. WHAT IS A PREDICATE?

A **predicate** is a word which defines or describes the subject of a sentence to which it is connected by a linking verb. Depending on whether it is a noun or adjective which follows the linking verb it is called a **predicate noun** or **predicate adjective.**

IN ENGLISH

The most frequent linking verb is *to be*. Other commonly used linking verbs include *to seem, to appear, to become, to taste* and *to feel*. By identifying the part of speech of the word that follows the linking verb, you can identify the type of predicate it is.

links *Natasha* to *girl*

Natasha *is* a foolish **girl.**

predicate noun

links *Natasha* to *foolish*

Natasha *is* **foolish.**

predicate adjective

links *mother* to *ill*   links *he* to *soldier*

Nikolai's mother *felt* **ill** when he *became* a **soldier.**

predicate adjective   predicate noun

Not all linking verbs perform that function all the time. The verb *to grow*, for example, may also be used intransitively without a predicate or transitively (see p. 74).

linking verb   She *grew* impatient.

describes subject *she*

intransitive verb   The beans *grew* slowly.

no direct object (*slowly* is an adverb)

transitive verb   She *grew* beans.

direct object

IN RUSSIAN

Predicates operate in much the same way as they do in English. Linking verbs take predicates either in the nominative or in the instrumental case (see **What is Meant by Case?**, p. 14). The choice of case is determined by the verb. Consult your textbook to learn the conditions for each case.

Predicates agree with the noun they modify, i.e., the subject, in gender and number. The case of the predicate is dictated by the verb and its tense.

linking verb   predicate adjective

*She seemed **sad.***
Она́ каза́лась **гру́стной.**

subject   linking verb   predicate adjective
fem. sing.   fem. sing.
                       instrumental case

linking verb   predicate noun

*He became an **engineer.***
Он стал **инжене́ром.**

subject   linking verb   predicate noun
masc. sing.   masc. sing.
                     instrumental case

linking verb   predicate noun

*Chekov is an extremely subtle **psychologist.***
Че́хов — тонча́йший **психо́лог.**

subject   linking verb omitted   predicate noun
masc. sing.   masc. sing.
                               nominative case

linking verb   predicate adjective

*The weather was **fine.***
Пого́да была́ **прекра́сная.**

subject   linking verb   predicate adjective
fem. sing.   fem. sing.
                     nominative case

As opposed to attributive adjectives, which stand before the word they modify, predicate adjectives always stand alone.

*You are a **free** man.*
Вы **свобо́дный** челове́к.

attributive predicate adjective   noun

*This man is **free.***
Этот челове́к **свобо́ден.**

predicate adjective

In all but the last example, the predicate adjectives are long form adjectives, i.e., their endings change to agree in number and case with the word they modify (see **What is a Descriptive Adjectives?**, p. 61).

Many Russian adjectives also have short forms, which can only be used if the adjective is in the predicate position. For some adjectives the short-form is optional, for others it is obligatory. Short-form adjectives agree in number and gender with the word they modify.

> *He is a very **busy** person.*
> Он о́чень **заня́той** челове́к.
>
> long-form, attributive adjective

> *He is very **busy** now.*
> Он сейча́с о́чень **за́нят**.
>
> short-form, predicate adjective

Simple comparative adjectives are another category of adjective which can only be used in the predicate position (see **What is Meant by Comparison of Adjectives?** p. 127). These forms are invariable, i.e., they do not change in gender, number or case.

> *This is my **older** brother*
> Это мой **ста́рший** брат.
>
> long-form, attributive adjective

> *My brother is **older** than I.*
> Мой брат **ста́рше** меня́.
>
> short-form, predicate adjective

▼▼▼▼▼▼▼▼▼▼▼▼▼▼▼REVIEW ▼▼▼▼▼▼▼▼▼▼▼▼▼▼▼▼▼▼

In the sentences below circle the predicate adjectives.
- Underline the predicate nouns.

1. You are most kind.

2. He is a very busy doctor.

3. Is the doctor busy now?

4. My older brother is a professor.

5. Is your brother younger or older than you?

10. WHAT IS A PRONOUN?

A **pronoun** is a word used in place of a noun or another pronoun. It is used to refer to someone or something that has already been mentioned or implied. The word that the pronoun replaces and refers to is called the **antecedent.**

> *Liz* likes horses. *She* owns a beautiful horse.

In the example above, the pronoun *she* refers to the proper noun *Liz*. *Liz* is the antecedent of the pronoun *she*.

> Here is the *girl whom* the boy hit.

In the example above, the pronoun *whom* refers to the noun *girl*. *Girl* is the antecedent of the pronoun *whom*.

There are many different kinds of pronouns. In this handbook we will distinguish nine different categories of pronouns. Each type of pronoun will be discussed in detail in a separate section.

Personal pronouns → refer to people and things (see p. 36).

> ***They** read.*
> **Они** читáют.

> *Here is Ann. Help **her**.*
> Вот Áня. Помогúте **ей**.

> *Wine? Yes, I drink **it**.*
> Винó? Да, я **егó** пью.

Demonstrative pronouns → to point out or indicate persons or things (see p. 50).

> *Tell me about **this**.*
> Расскажú мне об **э́том**.

> *Which book do you want, **this** (one) or **that** (one)?*
> Какýю кнúгу ты хóчешь, **э́ту** úли **ту**?

Possessive pronouns → to show ownership or possession (see p. 44).

> *Whose horse is this? **Mine**.*
> Чья э́то лóшадь? **Моя́**.

> *Whose house is this? **Ours**.*
> Чей э́то дом? **Наш**.

Interrogative pronouns → to ask questions in a question sentence (see p. 54).

> *What is that?*
> **Что** э́то?

> *Whom did you see?*
> **Кого́** ты ви́дела?

Relative pronouns (identical in form to interrogative pronouns) → introduce subordinate clauses (see p. 106).

> *I don't know what that is.*
> Я не зна́ю, **что** э́то.

> *She didn't see who left.*
> Она́ не ви́дела, **кто** ушёл.

> *Here is the book which I am reading.*
> Вот кни́га, **кото́рую** я чита́ю.

Reflexive pronouns → refer back to the subject of the sentence and indicate the receiver of the action (see p. 115).

> *He hates himself.*
> Он ненави́дит **себя́**.

> *I bought myself a book.*
> Я купи́л **себе́** кни́гу.

> *Talk about yourselves.*
> Расскажи́те о **себе́**.

Intensive pronouns →strengthen and emphasize the person or object to which they refer (see p. 118).

> *She herself is to blame.*
> Она́ **сама́** винова́та.

> *From the director himself...*
> От **самого́** дире́ктора...

Indefinite pronouns → to refer to unidentified persons or things (see p. 120).

> *Did you speak with anyone?*
> Ты с **ке́м-нибудь** говори́ла?

> *Yes, I spoke with someone.*
> Да, я с **ке́м-то** говори́ла.

*Do you want **anything**?*
Ты **что-нибудь** хо́чешь?

Negative pronouns are the negative equivalents of indefinite pronouns. See **What are Indefinite and Negative Pronouns and Adverbs?**, p. 120.

Nobody is home.
Никого́ нет до́ма.

*Give him **nothing**.*
Ничего́ ему́ не дава́й.

▼▼▼▼▼▼▼▼▼▼▼▼▼▼REVIEW ▼▼▼▼▼▼▼▼▼▼▼▼▼▼▼▼

The following sentences contain different types of pronouns.
▪ Circle the pronouns.
▪ Draw an arrow from the pronoun to the antecedent, if identified.

1. Mary, will you help Ann? She has no clue how to change a tire.

2. The book itself isn't bad, but nobody read it.

3. "What is this?" — "Fudge. Mary made it herself."

4. Did anyone tell Mark about the book which he forgot.

5. Which is the best route to St. Petersburg?

6. I forgot my pen. May I borrow yours?

11. WHAT IS A PERSONAL PRONOUN?

A **personal pronoun** is a word used in place of a noun which refers to a person or thing.

> This is Mishka. *She* is my dog.
> Russian is a hard language for *me*.
> Listen to the music. *It* is Russian jazz.

In both English and Russian, the personal pronoun has different forms to show the pronoun's function in the sentence.

Personal Pronouns Used as Subjects

In the following example, personal pronouns are used as subjects (see **What is a Subject?**, p. 19).

> *He* drove, but *I* took the metro.
>> *Who* drove? Answer: He.
>> *He* is the subject of the verb *drove*.
>
>> *Who* took the metro? Answer: I.
>> *I* is the subject of the verb *took*.

IN ENGLISH

A different personal pronoun will be used depending on the person being referred to. Here is a list of the personal pronouns used as subjects. They are said to be in the **subjective case.**

Singular	Plural	
I	we	the person(s) speaking; *called 1st person*
you	you	the person(s) spoken to; *called 2nd person*
he, she, it	they	the person(s) or thing(s) spoken about; *called 3rd person*

As you can see, these pronouns have a different form for each person (or persons) to which they refer. Some personal pronouns also show whether they are singular or plural. *We* and *they* are plural pronouns, *I* and *he, she* and *it* are singular, *you* is the same form for both singular and plural.

IN RUSSIAN

As in English, pronouns used as subjects are in the subjective or nominative case (see **What is Meant by Case?**, p. 14). Although the case system is much more developed in Russian, understanding cases of pronouns in English can help us understand how cases work in Russian. Compare the subject pronouns of English and Russian:

ENGLISH subjective case		RUSSIAN nominative case
I	1st person singular *the person speaking*	я
you	2nd person singular familiar *the person spoken to*	ТЫ
he	3rd person singular	ОН
she	*the person or thing*	ОНá
it	*spoken about*	ОНó
we	1st person singular *the person speaking + others*	МЫ
you	2nd person plural *the persons spoken to*	ВЫ
they	3rd person plural *the persons or things spoken about*	ОНИ́

Let us look more closely at the two subject pronouns *you* and *it*. These two pronouns behave very differently in English and Russian. All the examples here will be subject pronouns but most of what we say about them will also apply to object pronouns.

"YOU"—ТЫ OR ВЫ
IN ENGLISH
There is only one 2nd person pronoun to address another person or persons, *you*. There is no difference between *you* when you are addressing one person (the singular *you*) and *you* when you are addressing more than one person (the plural *you*). For instance, if there are many people in a room and you ask aloud: "Are you coming with me?" the *you* could refer to one person or many.

Ivan, are *you* coming with me?
|
singular

Ivan and Sasha, are *you* coming with me?
|
plural

IN RUSSIAN

Russian distinguishes not only between the singular and plural form of *you,* but also between what is called the familiar *you* (**ты**) and the formal *you* (**вы**). Let us look at each form.

- Familiar *you:* **ты**

  The familiar form of *you* (**ты**) is used to address a member of one's family, a close friend, a child or a pet. It can only be used in the singular, that is, to address one person or animal.

  *Asya, what are **you** doing?*
  Ася, что **ты** де́лаешь?

  *Lara, where are **you** living?*
  Ла́ра, где **ты** живёшь?

- Formal *you:* **вы**

  The formal form of *you* (**вы**) is used as a singular to address a person you do not know very well, or someone to whom you want to show respect. It is always used when addressing an individual by the first name and patronymic, a polite form of address.

  *Excuse me, can **you** tell me what time it is?*
  Извини́те, **вы** не ска́жете, кото́рый час?

  *Alexander Nikolaevich, **you** are wrong!*
  Алекса́ндр Никола́евич, **вы** непра́вы!

Вы is always used when addressing more than one person, regardless of whether you would use the familiar in the singular or not.

  *Asya and Lara, are **you** ready?*
  Ася и Ла́ра, **вы** гото́вы?

  *Dear friends, **you** have helped me a great deal!*
  Дороги́е друзья́, **вы** мне о́чень помогли́!

When in doubt about whether to use the familiar or formal form, use the polite formal (**вы**) unless you are speaking to a child or an animal.

"IT"—OH OR OHÁ OR OHÓ
IN ENGLISH

The neuter pronoun *it* is used to replace the noun for any non-living thing, i.e., an object or an idea.

  Where is the pencil? *It* is lying on the table.
  What kind of an idea is that? *It*'s no good.
  Here is my dorm. *It* is new.

IN RUSSIAN

Every Russian noun has gender (see **What is Meant by Gender?,** p. 7). The pronoun which replaces a noun must indicate the gender of the noun to which it refers. Thus a pronoun will either be masculine, feminine, or neuter.

To choose the correct form of *it,* you must:

> 1. ANTECEDENT: Find the noun *it* replaces.
> 2. GENDER: Determine the gender of the antecedent.
> 3. SELECTION: Use the pronoun that corresponds to that gender.

Below you will find an example of each gender:

> *Where is the pencil?* ***It is lying on the table.***
> > 1. ANTECEDENT: *it* replaces *the pencil.*
> > 2. GENDER: **карандáш** is masculine.
> > 3. SELECTION: **он**, masc. sing.
>
> Где карандáш? **Он** лежи́т на столе́.
>
> *What kind of an idea is that?* ***It's no good.***
> > 1. ANTECEDENT:*it* replaces *the idea.*
> > 2. GENDER: **идéя** is feminine.
> > 3. SELECTION: **онá**, fem. sing.
>
> Что э́то за идéя? **Онá** плохáя.
>
> *Here is my dorm.* ***It is new.***
> > 1. ANTECEDENT: *it* replaces *the dorm.*
> > 2. GENDER: **общежи́тие** is neuter.
> > 3. SELECTION: **онó,** neut. sing.
>
> Вот моё общежи́тие. **Онó** нóвое.

Personal Pronouns Used as Objects

In the following examples a personal pronoun is used as an object (see **What are Objects?,** p. 24).

> Vanya saw *us.*
> > He saw *whom?* Us.
> > *Us* is the direct object of *saw.*
>
> Pasternak wrote *her.*
> > Pasternak wrote *to whom?* Her.
> > *Her* is the indirect object of *wrote.*

IN ENGLISH

Pronouns that occur as objects in a sentence are different from those used as subjects. When a pronoun is used as the direct or indirect object or as the object of a preposition in English we say that it is in the **objective case.**

He and *I* work at the institute.

subjects → personal pronouns in subjective case

They met *him* and *me* on Red Square.

direct objects → personal pronouns in the objective case

I sent *them* some books from Moscow.

indirect object → personal pronoun in the objective case

They're going to the circus with *you* and *her.*

objects of a preposition → personal pronouns in the objective case

Compare the subjective and objective cases of English pronouns:

Nominative	Objective
I	me
you	you
he	him
she	her
it	it
we	us
you	you
they	them

Especially in children's speech you will hear confusion in the use of the subjective and objective cases. Consider the following examples:

incorrect   *Him* and *me* are pals.

objective case

correct   *He* and *I* are pals.

subjective case

incorrect   She gave her and *I* a kiss.

subjective case

correct   She gave *her* and *me* a kiss.

objective case

incorrect   Who's there? It is *me*.
                                        |
                                  objective case

correct   Who's there? It is *I*.
                                        |
                                  subjective case

Confusion in the use of personal pronouns in Russian may be avoided if their functions in English are carefully distinguished.

IN RUSSIAN

Instead of a single objective case, there are five cases of pronouns which can be used for pronoun objects: genitive, dative, accusative, instrumental and prepositional cases. The use of these different cases corresponds to the use of the same cases of the nouns.

You will find a chart of personal pronouns in your textbook. Study these forms thoroughly to avoid errors; personal pronouns in different cases may differ very little in spelling.

Summary: To determine the form of a personal pronoun, here is a series of steps to follow:

1. ANTECEDENT—Find the antecedent of the pronoun (the noun it replaces) if there is one.

2. PERSON, GENDER, NUMBER—Determine the person, gender and/or number of the pronoun.

   ▪ If it is the 2nd person, be careful to distinguish between *you* sin gular/familiar and *you* plural or formal singular. Without a clear antecedent the choice of **ты** or **вы** may be optional; once you have chosen **ты** or **вы** you must use it consistently in the sen tence.

   ▪ If it is the 3rd person singular, remember that the gender of the pronoun must agree with the gender of the noun it replaces.

3. FUNCTION—Determine the function and corresponding case of the pronoun.

   subject → nominative case
   direct object → accusative case
   indirect object → dative case
   agent or means → instrumental case
   object of the preposition → case will vary

4. SELECTION—Choose the form of the pronoun which corresponds to the person, gender, number and case determined in steps 1 - 3.

Let us apply these steps to some sample sentences.

> **They** *live in Moscow.*
> 1. ANTECEDENT: none
> 2. PERSON/GENDER/NUMBER: 3rd person pl.
> 3. FUNCTION/CASE: subject → nominative case

Они живу́т в Москве́.

> *Ivan Ivanovich, Katya saw* **you** *on Nevsky Prospect.*
> 1. ANTECEDENT: Ivan Ivanovich
> 2. PERSON/GENDER/NUMBER: 2nd person formal sing. (the same as the plural form)
> 3. FUNCTION/CASE: direct object → accusative case

Ива́н Ива́нович, Ка́тя **вас** ви́дела на Не́вском проспе́кте.
Without the context "Ivan Ivanovich," there would be no way to determine whether *you* should be translated in the familiar singular (**тебя́**), the formal singular (**вас**) or the plural (**вас**).

> *Peter went for a walk with* **her** *in Gorky Park.*
> 1. ANTECEDENT: none
> 2. PERSON/GENDER/NUMBER: 3rd person fem. sing.
> 3. FUNCTION/CASE: object of preposition **с** *(with)*, which here takes instrumental case

Пётр гуля́л с **ней** в Па́рке и́мени Го́рького.[1]

---

[1] Personal pronouns which begin with a vowel (this category includes all 3rd person pronouns) normally add an **н-** when preceded by prepositions.

▼▼▼▼▼▼▼▼▼▼▼▼▼▼▼▼REVIEW ▼▼▼▼▼▼▼▼▼▼▼▼▼▼▼▼▼

I. In the space provided, fill in the English and Russian pronouns that correspond to the person and number indicated.

SUBJECT

PERSON NUMBER	ENGLISH	RUSSIAN
1. 1st sing.	_____	_____
2. 3rd sing. fem.	_____	_____
3. 3rd pl.	_____	_____
4. 2nd sing. familiar	_____	_____
5. 1st pl.	_____	_____
6. 3rd masc. sing.	_____	_____
7. 2nd pl. polite	_____	_____
8. 3rd neuter sing.	_____	_____

II. Write Russian pronouns that you would use to replace the words in Italics.

1. Viktoria Alexandrovna, will *you* pass the mushrooms? _____

2. *Katya* and *I* are out to lunch. _____

3. *Katya* and *Julie* are home. _____

4. Do *you* and *your wife* like beer? _____

5. Vanya, *you* must pick up your toys. _____

6. Professor Brodsky, are *you* ready? _____

7. *My children* are at school. _____

III. The sentences below all have inanimate subjects. Write the Russian pronoun that you would use to replace the subject.

1. The window is open? (*window* = окно́) _____

2. Where is my magazine? (*magazine* = журна́л) _____

3. The book is on the table? (*book* = кни́га) _____

4. Are the windows open? _____

5. The books are on the table. _____

12. WHAT IS A POSSESSIVE PRONOUN?

A **possessive pronoun** is a word which replaces a noun and which also shows who or what possesses that noun.

>Whose house is that? *Mine.*

Mine is a pronoun which replaces the noun *house* and which shows who possesses that noun.

IN ENGLISH

Possessive pronouns refer only to the person or thing which possesses, not to the object possessed.

>1. Is that your house? Yes, it is *mine.*
>2. Are those your books? Yes, they are *mine.*

The same possessive pronoun *mine* is used, although the object possessed is singular *(house)* in example 1 and plural *(books)* in example 2.

Here is a list of the English possessive pronouns:

mine	ours
yours	yours
his, hers, its	theirs

IN RUSSIAN

Russian grammar does not make a distinction between possessive pronouns and possessive adjectives; it refers to both as **possessive pronouns**. Textbooks of Russian for English speakers call these forms by various names: pronouns, adjectives, "special modifiers," etc.; the terminology varies from one textbook to another. Be sure that you understand what is meant in English by possessive pronoun and possessive adjective. Before you read further consult **What is a Possessive Adjective?**, p. 65.

Possessives—1st and 2nd Person, Singular and Plural

The possessives мой *(my/mine)*, твой *(your/yours,* familiar singular), наш *(our/ours)* and ваш *(your/yours,* formal singular and plural) change form to agree in case, number and gender with the nouns to which they refer. (To learn about familiar and formal forms see p. 37.)

To determine the form of the possessive here is a series of steps to follow:

1. ANTECEDENT/WORD MODIFIED—Find the possessive word and determine the noun that it replaces or modifies.

2. GENDER AND NUMBER—Determine the gender and/or number of the antecedent or the word it modifies.

3. FUNCTION—Determine the function and corresponding case of the possessive word.

> subject → nominative case
> direct object → accusative case
> indirect object → dative case
> agent or means → instrumental case
> object of the preposition → case will vary

4. SELECTION—Attach to the possessive word the ending which corresponds to the gender, number and case determined in steps 1-3.

Let us apply these steps to some sample sentences.

> *This is **my** car.*
> 1. WORD MODIFIED: *my* modifies *car,* **машина**
> 2. GENDER/NUMBER: **машина** is a fem. sing. noun.
> 3. FUNCTION/CASE: subject → nominative case
> Это **моя** машина.

> *This car is **mine**.*
> 1. ANTECEDENT: *car,* **машина**
> 2. GENDER/NUMBER: **машина** is a fem. sing. noun.
> 3. FUNCTION/CASE: subject → nominative case
> Эта машина **моя**.

> *I saw **your** children.*
> 1. WORD MODIFIED: *your* modifies *children,* **дети**
> Note: Without a context you cannot know whether *your* is singular/familiar, singular/formal or plural. We will give both forms.
> 2. GENDER/NUMBER: **дети** is a pl. noun.
> 3. FUNCTION/CASE: direct object → accusative case
> Я видела **твоих/ваших** детей.

> *These tickets are **yours**.*
> 1. ANTECEDENT: *tickets,* **билеты**
> Note: Without a context you cannot know whether *yours* is singular/familiar, singular/formal or plural. We will give both forms.
> 2. GENDER/NUMBER: **билеты** is a masc. pl. noun.
> 3. FUNCTION/CASE: subject → nominative case
> Эти билеты **твой/ваши**.

*That is **our** book.*
  1. WORD MODIFIED: *our* modifies *book,* **кни́га**
  2. GENDER/NUMBER: **кни́га** is a fem. sing. noun.
  3. FUNCTION/CASE: subject → nominative case
Это **на́ша** кни́га.

*That book is **ours**.*
  1. ANTECEDENT: *book,* **кни́га**
  2. GENDER/NUMBER: **кни́га** is a fem. sing. noun.
  3. FUNCTION/CASE: subject → nominative case
Эта кни́га **на́ша.**

As you can see the Russian sentences above use the same word and form for *my/mine, your/yours* and *our/ours.*

Possessives—3rd Person, Singular and Plural

The possessives **его́** *(his),* **её** *(her/hers),* and **их** *(their/theirs)* are invariable, that is, they never change form.

*This is **his** house.*
Это **его́** дом.

*Whose house is this? **His**.*
Чей э́то дом? **Его́.**

*He spoke about **her** cat.*
Он говори́л о **её** коте́.

*Is the cat yours? No. **Hers**.*
Кот твой? Нет. **Её.**

Careful

The possessives **его́**, **её** and **их** are identical in form to the accusative cases of the personal pronouns *he, she, it* and *they.* Be careful not to confuse these look-alike words.

*She loves **him**.*
Она́ лю́бит **его́**.
          |
        personal pronoun
        accusative case

*She loves **his** horse.*
Она́ лю́бит **его́** ло́шадь.
          |
        possessive
        modifies *horse*

I know **them**.
Я **их** зна́ю.
|
personal pronoun
accusative case

This house is **theirs**.
Этот дом **их**.
|
possessive
replaces *house*

Reflexive Possessive: "One's own"

IN ENGLISH

When the 3rd person singular *(his, her/hers, its)* or plural *(their/theirs)* possessives are used, two meanings are often possible:

Sam loves *his* wife.

    1. Sam loves *his own* wife.
    2. Sam loves *someone else's* wife.

My dog ate *her* bone.

    1. My dog ate *her own* bone.
    2. My dog ate *another dog's* bone.

The context of the sentence usually makes the meaning clear. Or else we can add words to clarify what we mean: *own, someone else's, another's.*

IN RUSSIAN

No such ambiguity is possible. Russian uses a separate possessive form to translate the idea of "one's own."

Свой, *one's own,* is fully declined; it changes form to show gender, number and case. It is translated as "his own," "her own," "its own" or "their own" depending on the gender and number of the noun or pronoun to which it refers.

Свой can only be used when the subject of the clause is also the "possessor" of the object (see **What are Sentences, Phrases and Clauses?,** p. 158).

- **свой** is optional in the 1st and 2nd person; its use is determined by context.

    *I love **my** mother.*

    1. Я люблю мать.

        omitted "my" is understood

    2. Я люблю **мою** мать.

        "my" possessive pronoun

    3. Я люблю **свою** мать.

        "my own"
        reflexive possessive pronoun

- **свой** is obligatory in the 3rd person.

    *He loves **his** wife.*

    1. Он любит **свою** жену.

        his own wife

    2. Он любит **его** жену.

        someone else's wife

Because English speakers are rarely conscious of ambiguity in their own language, they often forget to use **свой** where it is obligatory. Since a serious misunderstanding may result, study carefully the rules in your textbook on the use of **свой**.

Careful

The possessive modifier, which must be expressed in English, may be replaced by another construction or omitted in Russian.

1. Possessive modifiers are very often omitted in Russian when the context makes clear who the "owner" is.

    *I washed **my** hair.*
    Я вымыла—голову.

        мою/свою is omitted

    *He'll be right back. He forgot **his** briefcase.*
    Он сейчас вернётся. Он забыл—портфель.

        свой is omitted

2. In conversational Russian possessive modifiers may be replaced by the preposition **y** and the genitive case (see p. 93) of the pronoun or noun "possessor."

*I have lots of books in **my** room.*
У меня́ в ко́мнате мно́го книг.

*We have a good restaurant in **our** city.*
У нас в го́роде хоро́ший рестора́н.

▼▼▼▼▼▼▼▼▼▼▼▼▼▼▼REVIEW ▼▼▼▼▼▼▼▼▼▼▼▼▼▼▼▼

I. Below are sentences with possessive pronouns and possessive adjectives.
■ Circle the possessive pronouns.
■ Underline the possessive adjectives.

1. I have my book. Do you have yours?

2. Did your parents come? Ours stayed at home.

3. Her report was the best. Yes, hers was.

4. This jacket isn't mine. Is it his?

5. My dog is over there. Where is your dog?

II. Write the English equivalent(s) of these Russian possessive forms.

1. его́ _____

2. мой _____

3. наш _____

4. её _____

5. их _____

6. ваш _____

7. твой _____

13. WHAT IS A DEMONSTRATIVE PRONOUN?

A **demonstrative pronoun** is a word that replaces a noun that has been mentioned before. It is called demonstrative because it points out a person or thing. The word *demonstrative* comes from *demonstrate,* to point out, to show.

> *This* is bad, but *those* are even worse.

IN ENGLISH

The principal demonstrative pronouns are *this* and *that* in the singular and *these* and *those* in the plural.

We generally use *this* or *these* for person(s) or object(s) closer to the speaker and *that* or *those* for one(s) that are farther away.

> *These* are fine, but *those* are ugly.

When the contrast between a nearer and a farther demonstrative pronoun does not apply, English often prefers the more general *that* form.

> I don't know anything about *that.*

To help you recognize demonstrative pronouns, here is a paragraph where the demonstrative pronouns are in italics:

> Which books do you want? *These* are essays and *those* are novels. *This* is by Tolstoy and *that* is by Gogol. I recommend *this;* it's shorter than *that.* If you don't like any of *these,* I can show you *those.* But as for your choice, you'll have to decide *that* yourself. *That* is your problem.

Be careful to avoid confusion between demonstrative pronouns and 3rd person plural pronouns used as objects. The demonstrative pronoun carries an implied *-one* or *-ones* which can be added to the sentence.

> Of the three kinds of apples, I prefer *these (ones).*
> plural demonstrative pronoun

> Apples, huh! I don't like *them.*
> plural personal pronoun used as an object

IN RUSSIAN

Russian grammar does not make a distinction between demonstrative pronouns and demonstrative adjectives; it refers to both as demonstrative pronouns. Textbooks of Russian for English speakers call these forms by various names: pronouns, adjectives, "special modifiers," etc.; the terminology varies from one textbook to another. Be sure that you understand what is meant in English by demonstrative pronoun and demonstrative adjective. Before you read further, consult the section **What is a Demonstrative Adjective?**, p. 66.

Этот may be translated as *this* or *that* and is the more generally used form, especially when no contrast is involved.

Тот normally expresses *that* in a contrast involving a *this* or a *that*.

To determine the form of the demonstrative here is a series of steps to follow:

1. ANTECEDENT/WORD MODIFIED—Find the demonstrative word and determine the noun that it replaces or modifies.

2. GENDER AND NUMBER—Determine the gender and/or number of the antecedent or the word it modifies.

3. CASE—Determine the function and corresponding case of the demonstrative word.

> subject → nominative case
> direct object → accusative case
> indirect object → dative case
> agent or means → instrumental case
> object of the preposition → case will vary

4. SELECTION—Attach to the demonstrative word the ending which corresponds to the gender, number and case determined in steps 1-3.

Let us apply these steps to some sample sentences.

> demonstrative   demonstrative
> adjective   pronoun
> | |
> *This play is bad, but **that (one)** is good.*
>   1. WORD MODIFIED: *this → play,* **пьéса**
>   ANTECEDENT: *that (one) →play,* **пьéса**
>   2. GENDER/NUMBER: **пьéса** is a fem. sing. noun.
>   3. FUNCTION/CASE: subject → nominative case
> **Эта** пьéса плохáя, а **та** хорóшая.
> | |
> demonstrative   demonstrative

demonstrative
adjective
|

*What can you tell me about **these** books?*
1. WORD MODIFIED: *these* → *books,* книги
2. GENDER/NUMBER: книги is a fem. pl. noun.
3. FUNCTION/CASE: object of the prepositional о *(about),*
   which takes the prepositional case

Что ты мо́жешь сказа́ть об э́тих кни́гах?
|
demonstrative

The two examples below illustrate the opposition of English *that* to Russian э́тот when no contrast is expressed. Note also that in each example the demonstrative form refers to an unexpressed antecedent.

demonstrative
pronoun
|

*I don't know anything about **that**.*
1. ANTECEDENT: an unexpressed entire idea
2. GENDER/NUMBER: unstated antecedent is always neut. sing.
3. FUNCTION/CASE: object of the preposition о *(about),*
   which takes the prepositional case

Я ничего́ не зна́ю об э́том.
|
demonstrative

demonstrative
pronoun
|

*How much did you pay for **that**?*
1. ANTECEDENT: an unexpressed object
2. GENDER/NUMBER: unstated antecedent is always neut. sing.
3. FUNCTION/CASE: object of the preposition за *(for),*
   which here takes the accusative case

Ско́лько ты заплати́ла за э́то?
|
demonstrative

Careful

English frequently uses demonstrative pronouns in combination with the verb "to be" (*this is, those were, are these, will that be,* etc.). Russian uses a special indeclinable demonstrative form, э́то, to translate all expressions of this type. This construction is very common in Russian. Be sure to consult your textbook .

This is *a house;* **these are** *houses.*
Это дом; э́то дома́.

What will that be?
Что э́то бу́дет?

Whose books were these?
Чьи э́то бы́ли кни́ги?

▼▼▼▼▼▼▼▼▼▼▼▼▼▼REVIEW ▼▼▼▼▼▼▼▼▼▼▼▼▼▼▼▼

Below are sentences with demonstrative pronouns and demonstrative adjectives.
▪ Circle the demonstrative pronouns.
▪ Underline the demonstrative adjectives.

1. This little piggy went to market and that one stayed home.

2. We must resolve this problem before we talk about that.

3. I don't know anything about that.

4. If that is what you think about these students here, those over there

   are even more talented.

5. These apples are awfully big.

6. Those are awfully small apples.

14. WHAT IS AN INTERROGATIVE PRONOUN?

An **interrogative pronoun** is a word used in place of a noun to introduce a question. The word *interrogative* is related to *interrogate,* meaning to question.

IN ENGLISH
Different interrogative pronouns are used for asking about persons, their possessions and things.

> *Who* is in the room?
> refers to a person

> I see a dog. *Whose* is it?
> refers to the owner

> *What* is on the table?
> refers to a thing

The personal interrogative pronoun, like some personal pronouns in English, has different case forms (see **What is a Personal Pronoun?,** p. 36).

Who is the subjective form and is used for the subject of the sentence.

> *Who* wrote the book?
> subject   direct object

> *Who* will help you?
> subject   direct object

Whom is the objective form and is used for the direct object of the sentence and for the object of a preposition.

> *Whom* do you know here?
>   subject
> direct object

> From *whom* did you get the book?
>   subject
> object of the preposition *from*

You will sometimes hear *who* used incorrectly as an object. In colloquial English the two sentences above would be expressed as follows:

Who do you know here? → *Whom* do you know here?
subjective form used as an object

Who did you get the book from? → *Whom* did you get the book from?
subjective form used as object of the preposition

Incorrect use of interrogative pronouns in Russian can often be traced back to their incorrect usage in English. It is important that you be able to distinguish *who* used correctly as a subject from *who* used as a colloquial substitute for the object *whom*.

Whose is the possessive form of *who* and is used to ask about possession and ownership.

I found a pen. *Whose* is it?
I have Sasha's book. *Whose* do you have?

What is the interrogative pronoun used to ask about things. It does not change form, regardless of its function in the sentence.

What is in the chest?
subject

What are you doing?
direct object

IN RUSSIAN
Russian grammar does not always make a distinction between interrogative pronouns and interrogative adjectives; it refers to both as interrogative pronouns. Be sure that you understand what is meant in English by interrogative pronoun and interrogative adjective. Before you read further, consult the section **What is an Interrogative Adjective?**, p. 67.

The three basic English interrogative words, *who?*, *what?* and *whose?* are translated into Russian in the following ways:

Who? (pronoun, no antecedent) → кто

Кто is always masculine singular regardless of the gender and number of the answer; the case depends on the function of *who* in the sentence.

> *Who was reading the newspaper?*
> Кто читáл газéту?

What? (pronoun or adjective) → что, какóй or котóрый

1. pronoun, no antecedent

what? → что, is always neuter singular regardless of the gender and number of the answer; the case depends on the function of *what* in the sentence.

> *What was on the table?*
> Что бы́ло на столé?

2. adjective, agrees in gender, number and case with the noun it modifies

what? (which...?, what kind of...?) → какóй

> *What book are you reading?*
> Какýю кнíгу ты читáешь?

what? (which?, which one?) → котóрый

> *At what time are you leaving?*
> В котóром часý вы уезжáете?

Whose? → чей

Чей always agrees in gender and number and case with the noun it modifies.

> *Whose dog is this?*
> Чья э́то собáка?
> |
>   nom. fem. sing.

> *Whose are these books?*
> Чьи э́то кнíги?
> |
>   nom. pl.

Careful

While here we are talking only about interrogatives, you should be aware that кто, что and котóрый are also commonly used as relative pronouns (see **What is a Relative Pronoun?**, p. 106).

To determine the form of the interrogative here is a series of steps to follow:

1. ANTECEDENT/WORD MODIFIED—Find the interrogative word and determine the noun that it replaces or modifies.

2. GENDER AND NUMBER—Determine the gender and/or number of the antecedent or the word that it modifies.

3. CASE—Determine the function and corresponding case of the interrogative word.

> subject → nominative case
> direct object → accusative case
> indirect object → dative case
> agent or means → instrumental case
> object of the preposition → case will vary

4. SELECTION—Select the form which corresponds to the gender, number and case determined in steps 1-3.

Let us apply these steps to some sample sentences.

> **Who** *wants to go to the movies?*
> 1. ANTECEDENT: none
> 2. GENDER/NUMBER: **кто** is always masc. sing.
> 3. FUNCTION/CASE: subject → nominative case
> **Кто** хо́чет пойти́ в кино́?

> **What** *are you talking about?*
> 1. ANTECEDENT: none
> 2. GENDER/NUMBER: **что** is always neut. sing.
> 3. FUNCTION/CASE: object of the preposition **о** *(about)*, which takes the prepositional case
> О **чём** вы говори́те?

> **Whose** *books are these?*
> 1. WORD MODIFIED: *whose* → *books*, **кни́ги**
> 2. GENDER/NUMBER: **кни́ги** is a fem. pl. noun.
> 3. FUNCTION/CASE: subject → nominative case
> **Чьи** э́то кни́ги?

In the English sentence above *whose* is an adjective which modifies *books*. In the following English sentence, *whose* is a pronoun which replaces *books*. Note that in Russian the two sentences are identical.

Whose are these books?
1. ANTECEDENT: *books* → **книги**
2. GENDER/NUMBER: **книги** is a fem. pl. noun.
3. FUNCTION/CASE: subject → nominative case

Чьи э́то кни́ги?

What [1] *book are you reading?*
1. WORD MODIFIED: *what* →*book,* **кни́га**
2. GENDER/NUMBER: **кни́га** is a fem. sing. noun.
3. FUNCTION/CASE: direct object → accusative case

Каку́ю кни́гу ты чита́ешь?

At **what** [1] *time (hour) are you leaving?*
1. WORD MODIFIED: *what* → *hour,* **час**
2. GENDER/NUMBER: **час** is a masc. sing. noun.
3. FUNCTION/CASE: object of the preposition **в** *(at),*
   which here takes the prepositional case

В **кото́ром** часу́ вы уезжа́ете?

---

[1]*What* is translated by **како́й** or **кото́рый** depending on context. Although textbooks of Russian make a distinction between these two pronouns (**како́й** asks for a description as in *what kind of?* and **кото́рый** asks for identification from among a limited group as in *which one?*), in practice **кото́рый** is used almost exclusively in questions about clock time.

▼▼▼▼▼▼▼▼▼▼▼▼▼▼▼REVIEW ▼▼▼▼▼▼▼▼▼▼▼▼▼▼▼▼▼

I. Below are sentences with interrogative pronouns and interrogative adjectives.
- Circle the interrogative pronouns.
- Underline the interrogative adjectives.

1. I can't hear you. What did you say about whose horses?

2. "Whose dog is this? To whom does it belongs?"

3. "At what time are you leaving?" "Who's asking?"

4. "Which wine do you prefer?" "I don't know what to say. I like all the wines which you serve me."

II. Write the English equivalent(s) of these Russian interrogative forms.

1. кто?   _____

2. что?   _____

3. который?   _____

4. чей?   _____

5. какой?   _____

III. Write the English equivalent of the interrogative forms in **boldface**.

1. **Что** ты говоришь?   _____

2. **Какой** журнал ты читаешь?   _____

3. **Который** час?   _____

15. WHAT IS AN ADJECTIVE?

An **adjective** is a word that modifies or describes a noun or pronoun. It answers the question *which one?*, *what kind?* or *how many?* Be sure that you do not confuse an adjective with a pronoun. A pronoun replaces a noun, while an adjective must always have a pronoun or noun to describe.

There are several different kinds of adjectives. In this handbook we will distinguish four categories of adjectives. Each type of adjective will be discussed in detail in a separate section.

Descriptive adjectives → describe qualities and characteristics of the noun they modify (see p. 61).

honest person	**че́стный** челове́к
sweet apple	**сла́дкое** я́блоко
large picture	**больша́я** карти́на

Possessive adjectives → show possession, that is, they answer the question *whose?* (see p. 65).

their problem	**их** пробле́ма
my goal	**моя́** цель

Demonstrative adjectives → point out or indicate the noun or pronoun they modify (see p. 66).

these boys	**э́ти** ма́льчики
that window	**э́то** окно́

Interrogative adjectives → ask questions about the noun or pronoun they modify (see p. 67).

which books?	**каки́е** кни́ги?
what time?	**кото́рый** час?
whose car?	**чья** маши́на?

IN ENGLISH
Adjectives do not change form, regardless of the case or number of the noun or pronoun they modify.

IN RUSSIAN
Adjectives must agree with the noun or pronoun they modify in gender, number and case.

16. WHAT IS A DESCRIPTIVE ADJECTIVE?

A **descriptive adjective** describes qualities or characteristics of the noun or pronoun it modifies. It is called an attributive or predicate adjective depending on how it is linked to the noun or pronoun (see **What is a Predicate?**, p. 30).

An **attributive adjective** usually precedes or, less commonly, comes immediately after the noun it modifies.

> The tsar lives in a *large* palace.
> > attributive adjective
> > modifies *palace*

> The house, *large* and *old,* was sold cheaply.
> > attributive adjectives
> > modify *house*

A **predicate adjective** follows a linking verb: *to be, seem, appear, become*, etc. (see p. 30). It refers back to the subject of the sentence.

> The apartment is *large.*
> > subject   predicate adjective

> The teacher seems *strict.*
> > subject   predicate adjective

IN ENGLISH
Descriptive adjectives, whether attributive or predicate adjectives, singular or plural, do not change form regardless of their function or the noun or pronoun they modify.

> The *cold* wind blew.
> attributive adjective
> modifies *wind,* the singular subject

> He threw me a *cold* look.
> > attributive adjective
> > modifies *look,* the singular direct object

I like *cold* winters.
|
attributive adjective
modifies *winters,* the plural direct object

Russian winters are *cold.*
|
predicate adjective
modifies *winters,* the plural subject

IN RUSSIAN

There are two types of adjectives, **long-form adjectives** and **short-form adjectives.**

A **long-form adjective** agrees in gender, number and case with the word it modifies.

A **short-form adjective** agrees in gender and number. It has only one form and does not decline.

Attributive adjectives can only be in the long form. These long-form adjectives agree in gender, number and case with the word they modify.

Predicate adjectives can be either in the long-form or in the short-form. The meaning of the adjective will be different depending on the form you use. Your textbook will clarify these differences.

Not all adjectives have a long-form and a short-form; study your textbook carefully. Adjectives are listed in the vocabulary section of your textbook and in the dictionary in the masculine singular nominative case form of the attributive adjective. That form ending must be removed to find the stem of the adjective on which to add other endings to agree with the noun or pronoun that the adjective modifies.

To choose the form of the adjective here are a series of steps to follow:

1. TYPE—Determine whether the adjective is an attributive or a predicate adjective.

   - If it is an attributive adjective, you will use the long-form adjective.

   - If it is a predicate adjective, you will have to determine whether you should use the long or the short-form adjective.

2. LONG-FORM—If you use the long-form adjective, determine the gender, number and case of the word it modifies.

   subject → nominative case (or for certain predicates the instrumental case, see p. 30)

direct object → accusative case
indirect object → dative case
agent or means → instrumental case
object of a preposition → case will vary

3. SHORT-FORM—If you use the short-form adjective, determine the gender and number of the word it modifies.

- If the word modified is singular, the adjective will reflect its gender.

- If the word modified is plural, the adjective will be plural.

4. SELECTION—Attach the proper ending based on the steps outlined above.

Let us apply these steps to some sample sentences.

*She lived in a **big** house.*
1. TYPE: *big* → attributive; adjective → long-form
2. GENDER/NUMBER: *house,* **дом,** is masc. sing.
3. FUNCTION/CASE: **дом** is the object of the preposition **в** *(in),* which here takes the prepositional case.

Она́ жила́ в **большо́м** до́ме.

*She was **glad** to see me.*
1. TYPE: *glad* → predicate adjective → short-form
   The predicate adjective *glad,* **рад,** is only short-form.
2. GENDER/NUMBER: *she,* **она́,** is fem. sing.

Она́ была́ **ра́да** меня́ ви́деть.

the fem. sing. ending **-a** agrees with **она́**

*The weather was **fine**.*
1. TYPE: *fine* → predicate adjective
   The predicate adjective for *fine* may be long-form or short-form.
2. GENDER/NUMBER: *weather,* **пого́да,** is fem. sing.
3. FUNCTION/CASE: **пого́да** is the subject of the sentence.

Пого́да была́ **хоро́шая.**

long-form adjective
the fem. sing. nominative case ending **-ая**
agrees with **пого́да**

Пого́да была́ **хороша́.**

short-form adjective
the fem. sing. ending **-a** agrees with **пого́да**

*She is writing to an **old** girlfriend.*
1. TYPE: *old* → attributive adjective → long-form
2. GENDER/NUMBER: *girlfriend,* **подру́га,** is fem. sing.
3. FUNCTION/CASE: **подру́га** is the indirect object→ dative case

Она́ пи́шет **ста́рой** подру́ге.

*She ate the soup with a **large** spoon.*
1. TYPE: *large* → attributive adjective → long-form
2. GENDER/NUMBER: *spoon,* **ло́жка** is fem. sing.
3. FUNCTION/CASE: **ло́жка** is the instrument of the action →
   instrumental case

Она́ е́ла суп **большо́й** ло́жкой.

*A **big** cat is sitting on the stairs.*
1. TYPE: *big* → attributive adjective → long-form
2. GENDER/NUMBER: *cat,* **кот,** is masc. sing.
3. FUNCTION/CASE: **кот** is the subject → nominative case

Большо́й кот сиди́т на ле́стнице.

Notice in the last three examples that the same adjectival ending -**ой** is used for three different cases. Case endings of adjectives in Russian must be studied very thoroughly to avoid confusion.

▼▼▼▼▼▼▼▼▼▼▼▼▼Review ▼▼▼▼▼▼▼▼▼▼▼▼▼▼▼▼

Circle the attributive adjectives in the sentences below.
▪ Underline the predicate adjectives.
▪ Draw an arrow from each adjective to the noun or pronoun described.

1. The young woman seemed sad.

2. The younger students are especially eager to learn.

3. I am tired after my morning run.

4. All international flights will be late.

17. WHAT IS A POSSESSIVE ADJECTIVE?

A **possessive adjective** is a word which describes a noun by showing who possesses it.

IN ENGLISH

Here is a list of the possessive adjectives:

my	our
your	your
his, her, its	their

English grammar makes a clear distinction between possessive adjectives and possessive pronouns (see **What is a Possessive Pronoun?**, p. 44). Although both show possession, they do so in different ways:

Possessive adjectives are used with the noun they modify and stand before the noun they modify

My horse likes carrots.

Possessive pronouns are used to replace a noun and stand after a verb.

This horse is *mine*.

IN RUSSIAN

Russian does not make a distinction between possessive adjectives and possessive pronouns. Russian grammar calls them both possessive pronouns; the same forms are used, regardless of whether the possessive modifies a noun or replaces it. Consult the Russian section of **What is a Possessive Pronoun?**, p. 44, for examples of possessives.

▼▼▼▼▼▼▼▼▼▼▼▼▼▼REVIEW ▼▼▼▼▼▼▼▼▼▼▼▼▼▼▼

[See Review for Possessive Pronouns, p . 49.]

18. WHAT IS A DEMONSTRATIVE ADJECTIVE?

A **demonstrative adjective** is a word used to point out a noun. The word *demonstrative* comes from *demonstrate,* to point out, to show.

IN ENGLISH
The principal demonstrative adjectives are *this, that, these* and *those.* They are a rare example of English adjectives agreeing with the noun they modify: before a plural noun *this* changes to *these* and *that* changes to *those.*

The distinction between *this* and *that* can be used to contrast one object with another; we generally say *this* (or *these)* for the closer object, and *that* (or *those)* for the one farther away.

> *These* books are mine and *those* books are his.
> referring to books at hand   referring to books further away

English grammar makes a clear distinction between demonstrative adjectives and demonstrative pronouns (see **What is a Demonstrative Pronoun?,** p. 50).

Demonstrative adjectives are used with the noun they modify and stand before the noun they modify.

> *This* horse is mine.

Demonstrative pronouns are used to replace a noun stand after a verb.

> Whose horses are *those?*

IN RUSSIAN
Russian does not make a distinction between demonstrative adjectives and demonstrative pronouns. Russian grammar calls them both demonstrative pronouns; the same forms are used, regardless of whether the demonstrative modifies a noun or replaces it. Consult the Russian section of **What is a Demonstrative Pronoun?,** p. 50, for examples of demonstratives.

▼▼▼▼▼▼▼▼▼▼▼▼▼▼REVIEW ▼▼▼▼▼▼▼▼▼▼▼▼▼▼▼
[See Review for Demonstrative Pronouns, p. 53.]

19. WHAT IS AN INTERROGATIVE ADJECTIVE?

An **interrogative adjective** is a word which asks a question about a noun.

IN ENGLISH

The words *which, what* and *whose* are called interrogative adjectives when they come before a noun and are used to ask a question .

> *Which* book do you want?
> *What* dress do you want to wear?
> *Whose* book is on the table?

English grammar makes a clear distinction between interrogative adjectives and interrogative pronouns (see **What is an Interrogative Pronoun?**, p. 54). Although both ask questions, they do so in different ways:

Interrogative adjectives are used with the noun they modify and stand before the noun they modify.

> *Whose* horse is that?
> *Which* horse will you ride?
> *What* breed of horse do you like?

Interrogative pronouns are used to replace a noun or pronoun and stand before a verb.

> *Who* said you could ride my horse?
> *What* do you know about horses?
> That is a nice horse. *Whose* is it?

IN RUSSIAN

Russian does not make a distinction between interrogative adjectives and interrogative pronouns. Russian grammar calls them both interrogative pronouns; different forms are used, however, depending on whether the interrogative modifies a noun or replaces it. Consult the Russian section of **What is an Interrogative Pronoun?**, p. 54, for examples of interrogatives.

▼▼▼▼▼▼▼▼▼▼▼▼▼▼▼REVIEW ▼▼▼▼▼▼▼▼▼▼▼▼▼▼▼▼▼
[See Review for Interrogative Pronouns, p. 59.]

20. WHAT IS A VERB?

A **verb** is a word (or group of words) that expresses an action, mental state or condition. The action can be physical, as in such verbs as *run, walk, climb, sing,* or mental, as in such verbs as *dream, believe,* and *hope.* Verbs like *be* and *become* express a state or condition rather than an action.

The verb is one of the most important parts of speech; you usually cannot express a complete thought, i.e., write a complete sentence (see p. 158), without a verb.

To help you learn to recognize verbs, here is a paragraph where the verbs are in italics:

> Arina Petrovna *sank* heavily into her chair, her eyes *staring* at the window. For the first minute she *seemed stunned* by the news. *Had* she *been told* that Stepan Vladimirovich *had committed* murder, or that the Golovlyovo peasants *had rebelled* and *refused* to *work* for her, or that serfdom *was toppling,* she *would have been* less *impressed.* Her lips *moved,* her eyes *looked* into the distance, but she *saw* nothing. She *did* not even *see* the girl Dunyasha *make* a dash past the window, *covering* something with her apron, then *whirl* around, on suddenly *seeing* her mistress, and slowly *walk* back (at another time such behavior *would have led* to a proper investigation). At last, however, Arina Petrovna *recovered* and *said:* "That's a nice thing to *do.*"
>
> (Mikhail Saltykov-Shchedrin, *The Golovlyovs*)

Terms to Talk About Verbs

INFINITIVE—A verb form starting with "to" is called an infinitive: *to eat, to sleep, to drink* (see **What is an Infinitive?,** p. 71).

CONJUGATION—A verb conjugates or changes in form to agree with its subject: *I do, he does* (see **What is a Verb Conjugation?,** p. 72).

TRANSITIVE OR INTRANSITIVE—A verb may be transitive, that is, take a direct object, or intransitive, that is, not take a direct object (see **What are Transitive and Intransitive Verbs?,** p. 74).

transitive	I *am reading* an interesting book.
	direct object
intransitive	I *work* in a factory.

TENSE—A verb indicates tense, that is, the time (present, past or future) of the action (see **What is Meant by Tense?**, p. 78).

present	*She works.*
past	*He worked.*
future	*They will work.*

ASPECT—A Russian verb also reflects a concept called aspect, an attitude toward time. It is extremely important to an understanding of the similarities and differences between the system of verbs in English and Russian (see **What is Meant by Tense?**, p. 78).

VOICE—A verb shows voice, that is, the relation between the subject and the action of the verb. A verb is in the active voice when the subject performs the action; it is in the passive voice when the subject is being acted upon (see **What is Meant by Active and Passive Voice?**, p. 131).

active	My friend *is building* a house.
passive	The house *is being built* by my friend.

MOOD—A verb shows mood, that is, the speakers' attitude toward what they are saying. English and Russian distinguish three moods:

1. **indicative** → for factual statements (see **What is the Present Tense?**, p. 82; **What is the Past Tense?**, p. 85; **What is the Future Tense?**, p. 89).

   She *studies* in the library.
   She *studied* in the library.
   She *will study* in the library.

2. **imperative** → for commands (see **What is the Imperative?**, p. 137).

   Come here!
   Rise and *shine!*

3. **subjunctive** (English) or **conditional** (Russian) → for statements which are hypothetical or contrary-to-fact (see **What are the Subjunctive and Conditional?**, p. 141).

   If you *would give* me the money, I *would buy* a car.
   Oh, how I *would like* to quit my job!

PARTICIPLE—A verb may also be used to form a participle, a word which looks like a verbal form and behaves like an adjective (see **What is a Participle?,** p. 145).

> I know the boy *reading* the book.
>> The participle *reading* shows an action (verb function) and describes a noun, *boy* (adjective function).

GERUND—In English there is a verbal noun (gerund), a word which looks like a verbal form and behaves like a noun (see **What is a Gerund?,** p. 153).

> *Reading* is my favorite pastime.
>> The gerund *reading* is formed from the verb *to read* (verb function) and it is the subject of the sentence (noun function).

21. WHAT IS AN INFINITIVE?

An **infinitive** is the name of the verb. It is under the infinitive form that you will find a verb in the dictionary.

IN ENGLISH
The infinitive is composed of two words: *to* + the dictionary form of the verb (*to speak, to dance*); this form, without the *to,* is sometimes called the **bare infinitive** (*speak, dance*). Although it is the most basic form of the verb, the infinitive can never be used in a sentence without another verb.

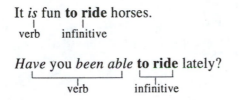

IN RUSSIAN
The infinitive, the dictionary form of the verb, expresses in a single word the English two-word infinitive. Most, but not all, infinitives end in **-ть**.

Most Russian verbs have two infinitives, one for the imperfective aspect and one for the perfective aspect (see **What is Meant by Tense?**, p. 78). You will therefore have to memorize two Russian infinitives for each English infinitive. As a rule verb lists give the imperfective infinitive first, followed by a slash and the perfective infinitive (if there is one).

Imperfective infinitive	Perfective infinitive	infinitive
писáть	написáть	*to write*
решáть	решúть	*to decide/solve*
переводúть	перевестú	*to translate*

22. WHAT IS A VERB CONJUGATION?

A **verb conjugation** is a list of the six possible forms of the verb, one for each of the subject pronouns (1st, 2nd and 3rd persons, singular and plural). Conjugations are always memorized with pronouns.

IN ENGLISH

Verbs change very little in form as they conjugate. Let us look at the various forms of the verb *to love* in the present tense when each of the six possible pronouns is the performer of the action.

Singular

1st person	I love
2nd person	you love
3rd person	{ he loves
	she loves
	it loves

Plural

1st person	we love
2nd person	you love
3rd person	they love

As you can see the only change in the verb conjugation is the addition of the "-s" in the third person singular. Because English verbs change so little many English speakers do not understand the idea of conjugation.

The best way to see the idea of conjugation in English is in the present tense conjugation of the verb *to be*.

Singular

1st person	I am
2nd person	you are
3rd person	{ he is
	she is
	it is

Plural

1st person	we are
2nd person	you are
3rd person	they are

The conjugation changes from *am* (1 st per. sing.) to *are* (2nd per. sing. and all plural forms) to *is* (3rd per. sing.).

IN RUSSIAN

The word **conjugation** has two meanings. The first, as in English, refers to a list of the six possible forms of a verb. The second refers to the two main patterns used to conjugate verbs. A verb belongs to either the first conjugation or the second conjugation. When you learn a new verb be sure to learn to which conjugation it belongs.

Let us look at the present tense conjugation of the first conjugation *to work,* **рабóтать,** and the second-conjugation verb *to speak,* **говорúть.**

	First conjugation	Second conjugation
Singular		
1st person	Я рабóтаю	Я говорю́
2nd person	Ты рабóтаешь	Ты говорúшь
3rd person {	Он рабóтает	Он говорúт
	Онá рабóтает	Она говорúт
	Онó рабóтает	Оно говорúт
Plural		
1st person	Мы рабóтаем	Мы говорúм
2nd person	Вы рабóтаете	Вы говорúте
3rd person	Онú рабóтают	Они говоря́т

Unlike English, Russian has a different verb form for each of the subject pronouns. By looking at the ending of the verb we can tell the number and the person of the verb.

Careful

Although the conjugation of verbs in Russian is almost always predictable once you have learned a few simple rules, different textbooks of Russian use different rules to describe verbs and to explain their conjugation. This can be very confusing if you work from more than one textbook. You will need to study your text carefully to master the particular system of conjugation rules it uses; all verbal forms (all tenses, the infinitive, participles) will be formed according to these basic rules.

23. WHAT ARE TRANSITIVE AND INTRANSITIVE VERBS?

A verb which takes a direct object is called a **transitive verb** (see **What are Objects?**, p. 24). It is indicated by a "v.t." in the dictionary. By definition a transitive verb must take a direct object, which usually comes after the verb.

He **will** never **kill** *anyone* with a single word.
    └──┬──┘   └─┬─┘
    transitive verb   direct object

Ivan Denisovich **ate** his *soup* very slowly.
                  │   │
              transitive verb direct object

A verb which does not take a direct object is called an **intransitive verb**. It is indicated in the dictionary by a "v.i." By definition an intransitive verb cannot take a direct object.

We *shall leave* for Kharkov on the night train.
   └──┬──┘
   intransitive verb (no direct object)

Lenin *died* in 1924.
       │
  intransitive verb (no direct object)

Many verbs may be used both transitively and intransitively.

I *ate* my cabbage soup.
   │   │
transitive verb   direct object

I *ate* slowly.
   │
intransitive verb

Some verbs which are transitive (v.t.) in English are intransitive (v.i.) in Russian; they do not take a direct object (the object of the verb is not in the accusative case).

We ***believe*** *you*.
     │   │
    v.t.   direct object
Мы **ве́рим** вам.
     │   │
    v.i.   dative case

He is avoiding me.
     | |
   v.t.   direct object

Он **избегáет** меня.
   | |
  v.i.   genitive case

▼▼▼▼▼▼▼▼▼▼▼▼▼▼▼▼REVIEW ▼▼▼▼▼▼▼▼▼▼▼▼▼▼▼▼▼▼

In the sentences below circle whether the verb is transitive (v.t.) or intransitive (v.i.).

■ Underline the direct object in sentences with a transitive verb.

1. I study Russian every night.   V.T.   V.I.

2. I live in Moscow.   V.T.   V.I.

3. I got dressed.   V.T.   V.I.

4. I dressed my child.   V.T.   V.I.

5. I returned the books.   V.T.   V.I.

6. We met last night at the station.   V.T.   V.I.

7. We met friends at the station.   V.T.   V.I.

24. WHAT IS A REFLEXIVE VERB?

A **reflexive verb** is a verb conjugated with a pronoun object used to reflect the action of the verb back to the performer, that is, the subject of the sentence. The result is that the subject of the sentence and the object are the same person.

IN ENGLISH

Reflexive verbs are conjugated with reflexive pronouns (see **What is a Reflexive Pronoun?,** p. 115). Reflexive verbs in English are transitive, that is, they take a direct object, the reflexive pronoun.Observe their usage in the following examples.

subject and object are the same person

I cut *myself.*

reflexive pronoun

subject and object are the same performer

The cat washed *himself.*

reflexive pronoun

IN RUSSIAN

Reflexive verbs are always intransitive, that is, they do not take a direct object. The particle -**ся** (-**сь** after vowels), a contraction of the reflexive pronoun **себя,** *oneself* (see p. 116), is attached to the verb to form the reflexive verb.

The cat washed himself.

reflexive verb + reflexive pronoun

Кот **умыва́лся.**

reflexive verb + reflexive particle

Careful

1. A reflexive verb in English is not always translated with a reflexive verb in Russian. The opposite is also true.

   Some English reflexive verbs are not reflexive verbs in Russian; therefore they do not add the reflexive particle. The Russian translation of these verbs will be a construction exactly parallel to the English: the verb and a reflexive pronoun.

*He **loves** only **himself.***
reflexive   reflexive
verb   pronoun

Он **лю́бит** то́лько **себя́**.
verb   reflexive pronoun

Some verbs in English may imply, but not express, a reflexive pronoun, whereas in Russian the reflexive particle will be stated.

I am dressing. [*myself* is implied]
Я одева́ю**сь**.
reflexive particle expressed

Please sit down. [*yourself* is implied]
Сади́те**сь**, пожа́луйста.
reflexive particle expressed

2. Some verbs may be used in both reflexive and non-reflexive forms.

I *am washing.* [*myself* is implied]
Я **мо́юсь**.
reflexive verb

*I **am washing** the dishes.*
Я **мо́ю** посу́ду.
non-reflexive verb

3. Verbs with the particle **-ся** are not always reflexive in meaning.

*He **seemed** sad.*
Он **каза́лся** гру́стным.

*She **laughs** a lot.*
Она́ мно́го **смеётся**.

*I **am afraid** of dogs.*
Я **бою́сь** соба́к.

The particle **-ся** is also used to form passive constructions (see **What is Meant by Active and Passive Voice?**, p. 131).

25. WHAT IS MEANT BY TENSE?

The **tense** of a verb indicates when the action of the verb takes place. The word for tense comes from the Latin *tempus* (from which we get the words tempo, temporal, temporary) meaning *time*. The three basic tenses are:

present	I eat.
past	I ate.
future	I will eat.

As you can see in the examples above, just by putting the verb in a different tense and without any additional information (such as "I am eating *now,*" "I ate *yesterday,*" "I will eat *tomorrow*"), you can indicate when the action of the verb takes place: now, before now, or after now.

Although we can identify a past, present and future tense in both English and Russian, these identically named tenses do not always have the same meanings.

IN ENGLISH

By using auxiliary verbs (such as *have, do, are*) and participles (see **What is a Participle?**, p. 145) English can create many tenses. Look at the following tenses and their names; these are the tenses you will most often encounter in translating to and from English and Russian. The six principal tenses of English are in boldface.

present	I cook
present progressive	I am cooking
present perfect	I have cooked
present perfect progressive	I have been cooking
present emphatic	I do cook
past	I cooked
past progressive	I was cooking
past perfect	I had cooked
past perfect progressive	I had been cooking
past emphatic	I did cook
future	I will cook
future progressive	I will be cooking
future perfect	I will have cooked
future perfect progressive	I will have been cooking

IN RUSSIAN

Russian verbs have only three tenses: past, present and future. These three tenses correspond to one of several different tenses in English, depending upon context.

present	Я рабо́таю	*I work* *I am working* *I have worked* *I have been working* *I do work*
past	Я рабо́тал	*I worked* *I have worked* *I was working* *I had been working* *I used to work* *I would work* *I did work*
future	Я бу́ду рабо́тать	*I will work* *I will be working* *I will have been working*

In addition to three tenses, Russian verbs have two **aspects**. Very crudely defined, aspect is an attitude toward action in time:

action as process → **imperfective aspect**
action as completion → **perfective aspect**

When you first begin to study verbs you will learn only one aspect: the infinitive (or some other form) of the imperfective aspect. Using this form you will derive the present, past and future tenses. The perfective aspect will be introduced later in your study. From then on you will have to learn two forms (one for the imperfective aspect and one for the perfective aspect) for each verb. Verb lists give the imperfective form first, followed by a slash and the perfective form (see p. 71).

Imperfective Aspect

Using an imperfective aspect verb you can form the present tense (which is only formed from imperfective verbs), the past tense and the future tense. You use imperfective aspect verbs to form past and future tenses when you want to emphasize:

▪ repeated or habitual actions

I *worked* every day on my Russian.
I always *did* my homework.
We *will* never *smoke*.
He *would* only *buy* vodka on Saturdays.

- actions in progress and therefore incomplete

> I *was working* when he came in.
> *Will* you *be working* when I come?

- actions which do not terminate in a result

> I *lived* and *worked* in Moscow.
> We *went walking* in the woods yesterday.

- completed actions which do not emphasize a result

> What *did* you *do* yesterday? [what activity took place?]
> —We *watched* soccer on T.V. [emphasis on activity]
> —And I *read* the newspaper. [emphasis on activity]

Perfective Aspect

Using a perfective aspect verb you can form the past tense and the future tense. You use perfective aspect verbs to form past and future tenses when you want to emphasize:

- single or momentary actions

> I *broke* the vase.
> I *shall read* the book and *return* it right away.

- actions which emphasize the goal of completion

> *Did* you *finish writing* your term paper?
> *Will* she *memorize* her part?
> When *will* you *begin?* I already *began.*
> What *did* you *do* yesterday? [what was accomplished?]
> —We *watched* a soccer match on T.V. [specific event]
> —And I *read* Brodsky's latest book. [specific event]

Look at the following examples which contrast imperfective and perfective aspect. Notice that in English aspect is often conveyed with the help of words and phrases which express an attitude toward time. When you are trying to decide what aspect to use to translate an English past or future tense verb, pay careful attention to these clues which will guide you to the correct choice.

> *I read every day.*
> "Read" alone may express either process or completion.
> *Every day* emphasizes a habitual, regular action
> Я **читáл** кáждый день.
> |
> imperfective aspect verb
> expresses action as duration of process

*I **read** the entire book.*
"Read" alone may express either process or completion.
Entire clarifies the action as result-oriented

Я **прочита́л** всю кни́гу.
    |
perfective aspect verb
expresses a complete and completed action

You will find a more detailed discussion of tense and aspect in the following sections: **What is the Present Tense?**, p. 82; **What is the Past Tense?**, p. 85; **What is the Future Tense?**, p. 89.

26. WHAT IS THE PRESENT TENSE?

The **present tense** indicates that the action is going on at the present time.

IN ENGLISH

There are five types of present tense; although each has a slightly different meaning, all indicate that the action is going on at the present time. For a native speaker of English, the choice of a present tense is virtually automatic, but as the sentences below illustrate, that choice is not optional. Each tense conveys a different meaning and emphasis.

> Where *does* Mary study?
> Mary *studies* in the library.
>
> Where *is* Mary now?
> Mary *is studying* in the library.
>
> *Does* Mary *study* in the library?
> Yes, she *does* (*study* in the library).

The **present** (sometimes called the **simple present**) tense → for habitual actions and general statements.

> I *ride* my horse every day.
> Pushkin's stories *are* very clever.

The **present progressive** tense → for actions in progress which emphasize that the action is going on now.

> Sinyavsky *is working* on a new novel.

The **present perfect** tense → for actions begun in the past and continuing in the present or for actions which have occurred at an unspecified time in the past.

> I *have lived* in Moscow for nine years.
> I *have read* most of Babel's stories.

The **present perfect progressive** tense → for actions begun in the past which are likely to continue in the future.

> I *have been living* near Red Square for several years.

The **present emphatic** tense → for emphasis, negative statements and questions.

> I really *do like* Tchaikovsky.
> I *don't like* Shostakovich.
> *Do* you *like* Glinka?

IN RUSSIAN
There is only one verb form to indicate the **present** tense; it can only be formed from imperfective aspect verbs.

Be sure to read the section on aspect in **What is Meant by Tense?**, p. 78 before you read further. The present tense in Russian corresponds to the English simple present, present progressive, present perfect progressive and present emphatic tenses.

> *I **live** in Moscow.*
> *I **am living** in Moscow.*   Я **живу́** в Москве́.
> *I **have been living** in Moscow.*
> *I **do live** in Moscow.*

Except for verbs of motion, in Russian the present tense describes:

- an action in progress

> Я **сейча́с** чита́ю э́то письмо́.
> *I **am reading** that letter right now.*

- a habitual action

> Я **пишу́** друзья́м раз в ме́сяц.
> *I **write** to my friends once a month.*

- a potential action

> Ма́ша уже́ **чита́ет**.
> *Masha already **reads**.*

Careful
With one exception all the present tenses of English verbs may be translated into Russian by the present tense. The exception is the present perfect tense *(I have lived)*.The present perfect tense translates into Russian with the present tense only if the context implies that the action is continuing at the present time.

> *I **have** already **lived** in Moscow **for two years**.*
> ┗━━━━━┯━━━━━┛   │
>   present perfect tense
>   "for two years" shows the action is continuing in the present.
>
> Я **живу́** в Москве́ уже́ два го́да.
>   │
>   present tense

When the action of a present perfect verb does not continue in the present, it is translated by the past tense (see **What is the Past Tense?**, p. 85). In the sentence below the action of the verb indicates a past action which is no longer taking place in the present.

*I **have lived** in Moscow.*
└──┬──┘
present perfect tense

Я **жила́** в Москве́.
│
past tense, imperfective aspect

▼▼▼▼▼▼▼▼▼▼▼▼▼▼▼▼▼▼REVIEW ▼▼▼▼▼▼▼▼▼▼▼▼▼▼▼▼▼▼▼

I. The following are questions in the present tense.
- Fill in the proper form of the verb *to read* in the answers.

1. What does Mary do all day?

   She _____

2. Has she read War and Peace?

   No, but she_____it right now.

3. Does Mary read Russian?

   Yes, she _____Russian.

II. The verbs in the following sentences are in the present perfect tense.
- Indicate the name of the tense you would use to translate into Russian each verb in *italics*.

1. We *have studied* at the institute for three years.   _____

2. I *have* already *met* him.   _____

3. *Have* you *worked* there long?   _____

4. I *have worked* there.   _____

5. I *have* never *studied* this problem.   _____

27. WHAT IS THE PAST TENSE?

The **past tense** is used to express an action that occurred previously, at some time in the past.

IN ENGLISH
There are five past tenses; although each has a different meaning, all past tenses show that an action has occurred at some time in the past.

The **past** (sometimes called the **simple past**) tense → for a single or repeated action that has been completed. It is the only past tense made up of one word.

Tolstoy *went* to the Caucasus.

The **past progressive** tense → for emphasizing the duration of a past action, often related to another, simultaneous actlon.

When I saw him, he *was hurrying* to class.

The **past perfect** tense → for emphasizing the completion of a past action, often before the beginning of another action.

Chekhov *had died* by the time Gorky became famous.

The **past perfect progressive** tense → for a past action that continued until the onset of another action.

I *had been feeling* ill until I went to the polyclinic.

The **past emphatic** tense → for emphasis, negative statements and questions.

I *did hope* to see the mausoleum in Moscow.
I *did*n't *do* anything yesterday.
What *did* you *do* today?

Additionally the **present perfect** tense may also convey a past action which is no longer in force.

IN RUSSIAN
A typical Russian verb has two past tenses, one formed from its imperfective aspect and the other from its perfective aspect. Be sure to read the section on aspect in **What is Meant by Tense?**, p. 78, before you read further.

Let us look at some English sentences with past tense verbs that are translated with the imperfective aspect. Expressions of time or other key words that show an attitude toward time play a decisive role in dictating the choice of aspect.

> *Formerly I **wrote** a lot.*
> emphasizes that the action was frequently repeated
> Ра́ньше я мно́го **писа́ла**.

> *When I entered, he **was writing**.*
> past progressive tense
> All progressive tenses emphasize action in progress and are always translated with the imperfective aspect.
> Когда́ я вошла́, он **писа́л**.

> *Yesterday he **wrote** all day.*
> emphasizes the duration of an action
> Вчера́ он **писа́л** весь день.

> *I **wrote** this book for three years.*
> the action continued for three years; whether or not the action was completed is not stated
> Я **писа́ла** э́ту кни́гу три го́да.

Now let us look at some English sentences with past-tense verbs that are translated with the perfective aspect. Here, too, time expressions or other key words help to show which aspect to use.

> *They **wrote** all the letters.*
> emphasizes a concrete, result-oriented action
> Они́ **написа́ли** все пи́сьма.

> *I **wrote** the book in (within) three years.*
> indicates that the entire action was completed within a well-defined time period.
> Я **написа́л** э́ту кни́гу за три го́да.

> *I just **wrote** the letter.*
> adverbs emphasize the completion of an entire action
> Я то́лько что **написа́ла** письмо́.

Careful

All but one of the English sentences in the examples above contain the verb *wrote*. The simple past tense (*I wrote*) may be translated into Russian using an imperfective aspect verb or a perfective aspect verb. It is context which determines the choice of aspect.

Without expressions of time or other key words that show an attitude toward time the meaning of the simple past tense is ambiguous and the verb may be translated into Russian with either aspect. From the perspective of Russian, however, the imperfective and perfective aspects are not interchangeable; their meanings are very different.

Look below at the two translations of the sentence "I read the book."

In the first translation using the imperfective aspect, the fact of the action is stated, but there is no indication of the result. The speaker indeed may have finished reading the book, but that is not pertinent.

> *I **read** the book.*
> Я **читáл** кни́гу.
> |
>   past tense
>   imperfective aspect

In the second translation using the perfective aspect, the speaker focuses on and emphasizes the completion of the action, that the entire book was read.

> *I **read** the book.*
> Я **прочитáл** кни́гу.
> |
>   past tense
>   perfective aspect

▼▼▼▼▼▼▼▼▼▼▼▼▼▼▼▼REVIEW ▼▼▼▼▼▼▼▼▼▼▼▼▼▼▼▼▼▼

I. Here are two English verbs in their infinitive form.
- Fill in three (of the possible six) past-tense verb forms we can use in English to indicate that an action has already taken place.

1. to write   I   _____

                 I   _____

                 I   _____

2. to swim   she   _____

             she   _____

             she   _____

II. Do not attempt this exercise until you have studied aspect. The sentences below are all in the past tense.
- Indicate if the verb in *italics* would be translated into Russian with the imperfective aspect (I) or the perfective aspect (P).

1. What *were* you *doing* last night?   I   P

2. When he arrived, I *had* already *cooked* the dinner.   I   P

3. Until last week I *had been working* for an insurance firm.   I   P

4. He *would* often *buy* her flowers.   I   P

5. I *played* tennis yesterday.   I   P

6. I *played* two games of tennis yesterday.   I   P

7. I *wrote* the novel for a year.   I   P

8. I *wrote* the whole novel in a year.   I   P

28. WHAT IS THE FUTURE TENSE?

The **future tense** is used to describe an action which will take place in time to come, the future.

IN ENGLISH

There are four future tenses: although each has a different meaning, all future tenses show that an action will take place in time to come, the future.

The **future** (sometimes called **simple future**) tense → for a single or repeated future action.

> We *shall overcome* some day.

The **future progressive** tense → for a future action that will continue.

> What *will* you *be doing* this summer?

The **future perfect** tense → for a future action with a definite termination, that is, a completed action in the future.

> Our professor *will have graded* our exams by tomorrow.

The **future perfect progressive** tense → for a future action that will continue until some later point.

> By May I *will have been studying* Russian for a year.

IN RUSSIAN

A typical Russian verb has two future tenses, one formed from its imperfective and the other from its perfective aspect. Be sure to read the section on aspect in **What is Meant by Tense?**, p. 78, before you read further.

Let us look at some English sentences with future tense verbs that are translated with the imperfect aspect. Expressions of time or other key words that show an attitude toward time play a decisive role in dictating the choice of aspect.

> *They **will play** all day.*
>
> emphasizes the duration of an action
> Они весь день **бу́дут игра́ть.**

*They **will be working** here.*

future progressive tense
All progressive tenses emphasize action in progress and are always translated with the imperfect aspect.

Они **бу́дут рабо́тать** здесь.

*By May, we **will have been studying** Russian for a year.*

future perfect progressive
All progressive tenses emphasize action in progress and are always translated with the imperfect aspect.

К ма́ю, мы **бу́дем занима́ться** ру́сским языко́м уже́ год.

Now let us look at some English sentences with future tense verbs that are translated with the perfective aspect. Here, too, time expressions or other key words help to show which aspect to use.

*They **will return** the book.*

future
The book clarifies that the action is a single, momentary event.

Они **верну́т** кни́гу.

*I **will have learned** these words by supper.*

future perfect
"By supper" indicates a result-oriented action with a stated time of completion. English future perfect tenses always point to completion of the action; here the action will be completed at some time in the future.

Я **вы́учу** э́ти слова́ к у́жину.

Careful

In many instances, Russian is more strict than English in its use of tenses, especially in complex sentences (see **What are Sentences, Phrases and Clauses?**, p. 158).

1. While English uses the present tense after such expressions as *if, when, as soon as, by the time* which introduce an action that will take place in the future, Russian uses the future tense.

*If he **calls**, I will tell him.*

present
Если он **позвони́т**, я ему́ скажу́.

future
word-for-word "if he will call..."

*Will you tell me when she **calls**?*
|
present

Ты мне ска́жешь, когда́ она́ **позвони́т**?
|
future
word-for-word "when she will call..."

2. Sometimes Russian will use the present tense with an adverb of future time instead of using the future tense of the verb. We do this in English as well.

Я за́втра **е́ду** на Украи́ну.
| |
adverb present tense for future time
*Tomorrow I **am going** to Ukraine.*

The use of the future tense in this type of sentence adds emphasis (some obstacle has been overcome, a change of plans, etc.).

Я за́втра **пое́ду** на Украи́ну.
|
future tense
*Tomorrow I **shall go** to Ukraine.*

3. The simple future tense *(I will write)* may be translated into Russian using an imperfective aspect verb or a perfective aspect verb. It is context which determines the choice of aspect.

Without expressions of time or other key words that show an attitude toward time the meaning of the simple future tense is ambiguous and the verb may be translated into Russian with either aspect. From the perspective of Russian, however, the imperfective and perfective aspects are not interchangeable; their meanings are very different.

Look below at the two translations of the sentence "I will read the book."

In the first translation using the imperfective aspect, the fact of the action is stated, but there is no indication of the result. The speaker indeed may finish the book, but that is not pertinent.

Я бу́ду **чита́ть** кни́гу.
|
future tense
imperfective aspect

In the second translation using the perfective aspect, the speaker focuses on and emphasizes the completion of the action, that the entire book will be read.

Я **прочита́ю** кни́гу.

future tense
perfective aspect

▼▼▼▼▼▼▼▼▼▼▼▼▼▼▼REVIEW ▼▼▼▼▼▼▼▼▼▼▼▼▼▼▼▼

I. Here are two English verbs in their infinitive form.
- Fill in the four future tense verb forms we can use in English to indicate that an action will take place.

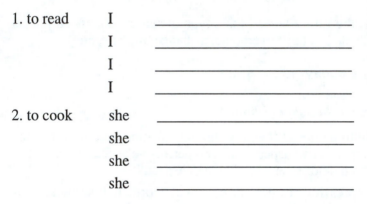

1. to read   I   _____

                    I   _____

                    I   _____

                    I   _____

2. to cook   she   _____

                    she   _____

                    she   _____

                    she   _____

II. Do not attempt this exercise until you have studied aspect. The sentences below are all in the future tense.
- Indicate if the verb in *italics* would be translated into Russian with the imperfective aspect (I) or the perfective aspect (P).

1. I *will write* to you everyday.   I   P

2. I *will study* Russian in the fall.   I   P

3. What *will* you *be doing* tomorrow?   I   P

4. "Did you call Nina?" "No, but I *will call* her right now."   I   P

5. "Did you finish the dishes yet?" "No, but I *will have finished* by the time you get home."   I   P

6. "What *shall* we *do* this evening?" "Let's relax."   I   P

7. *Will* you *return* this book to the library when you leave?   I   P

29. WHAT IS A PREPOSITION?

A **preposition** is a word which shows the relationship between a noun or pronoun and another word in the sentence. Prepositions commonly indicate position, direction, time or manner.

The noun or pronoun which the preposition connects to the rest of the sentence is called the **object of the preposition**. The preposition and its object together make up a **prepositional phrase.**

IN ENGLISH
Here are some common examples of prepositions:

- position

prepositional phrase
Misha studied *in* the library.
object of the preposition

prepositional phrase
The books are *on* the table.
object of the preposition

- direction

prepositional phrase
Varya went *to* the market.
object of the preposition

prepositional phrase
He came *from* Kiev yesterday.
object of the preposition

- time

prepositional phrase
I get up *at* 6:00 a.m.
object of the preposition

prepositional phrase
It is very cold here *in* January.
object of the preposition

▪ manner

prepositional phrase

They left *without* us.

object of the preposition

prepositional phrase

He writes *with* a pen.

object of the preposition

Not all prepositions are single words:

because of	in front of	instead of
due to	in spite of	on account of

To help you recognize prepositional phrases, here is a short text in which the prepositions are in **boldface** and the objects of the prepositions are in *italics*.

> The autumn was dry and warm. It gave us time to dig up the potatoes **before** *the rains and the cold weather*. Not counting those we gave back **to** *Mikulitsyn,* we had twenty sacks. We put them **in** *the biggest bin* **in** *the cellar* and covered them **with** *old blankets and hay*. We also put down two barrels **of** *salted cucumbers* and two **of** *sauerkraut* prepared **by** *Tonia*. Fresh cabbage hung **in** *pairs* **from** *the beams*…. There is enough firewood **in** *the shed* to last us **until** *Spring*. (Boris Pasternak, *Doctor Zhivago*)

IN RUSSIAN

Prepositions are invariable (that is, they never change form), but objects of prepositions decline or change form to reflect case (see **What is Meant by Case?,** p. 14).

When you memorize a preposition, you must also learn in which case to put its object. Be careful: some prepositions may take more than one case.

Prepositions are very tricky. Every language uses prepositions differently. Do not assume that the same preposition is used in Russian as in English. Sometimes phrases with prepositions in one language are expressed without prepositions in the other language.

1. Many prepositions which must be used in English are unnecessary in Russian because of the system of cases.

- The preposition of possession in English, *of,* is expressed in Russian by the genitive case, the case of possession.

      prepositional phrase   genitive case

the author **of** *the book* → áвтор **книги**

      prepositional phrase   genitive case

the house **of** *my friend* → дом **моегó дрýга**

- The indirect object (see p. 25) in English is often expressed using the preposition *to* or *for;* in Russian the indirect object is always expressed without a preposition by the dative case.

      prepositional phrase   dative case

a present **for** *brother* → подáрок **брáту**

      prepositional phrase   dative case

a letter **to** *a friend* → письмó **дрýгу**

- Prepositions which show manner, means or agent (*with, by, by means of*) in English are often expressed in Russian without a preposition by the instrumental case.

      prepositional phrase   instrumental case

I write **with** *a pen.* → Я пишý **рýчкой.**

      prepositional phrase   instrumental case

a letter written **by** *him* → письмó напи́санное **им**

2. Some verbs which are followed by a prepositional phrase in English are expressed without a preposition in Russian.

- "to be afraid *of...*" → **боя́ться** + genitive case

      prepositional phrase

I am afraid **of** *snakes.*

Я бою́сь **змей.**

    genitive case

■ "to be satisfied *with*... " → **быть дово́лен** + instrumental case

prepositional phrase

I am satisfied **with** *your work.*
Я дово́лен **ва́шей рабо́той**.

instrumental case

3. Some verbs which take a direct object in English are expressed in Russian with the help of a prepositional phrase.

■ "to approach" → **подойти́** + **к** + dative case

direct object

He approached *the door.*
Он подошёл **к две́ри**.

prepositional phrase

■ "to enter" → **войти́** + **в** + accusative case

direct object

She entered *the house.*
Она́ вошла́ **в дом**.

prepositional phrase

4. A preposition may have several different meanings. You must analyze its function before you can determine its translation. As an example let us look at a few of the several different meanings of the preposition *for:*

■ "to fetch" → **за** + instrumental case

*I am going **for** some milk.*
Я иду́ **за** молоко́м.

instrumental case

■ "in favor of" → **за** + accusative case

*I voted **for** her.*
Я голосова́л **за** неё.

accusative case

■ destination → **в** or **на** + accusative case

We are leaving for Ukraine, for Kiev.
Мы уезжа́ем **на** Украйну, **в** Ки́ев.
　　　　　　　　└──────┬──────┘
　　　　　　　　accusative case

5. The position of a preposition in an English sentence may vary. In colloquial English you will often hear sentences in which the preposition comes at the end of the sentence, far from its object; it is called a **dangling preposition** (see p. 110). Formal English always places the preposition before its object.

colloquial	He is the man I ate *with*.
formal	He is the man *with whom* I ate.
colloquial	That is the store I go *to*.
formal	That is the store *to which* I go.
colloquial	That is the hero I'm talking *about*.
formal	That is the hero *about whom* I'm talking.

The position of the preposition in Russian is the same as in formal English; that is, it always comes before its object; it is never at the end of a sentence.

When expressing an English sentence in Russian, remember to restructure any dangling prepositions. Then you will be able to see clearly the object of the preposition and put it in its proper case.

Who did you buy the book *for?* →
For whom did you buy the book?
Для кого́ ты купи́ла кни́гу?
object of the preposition **для**,
which takes the genitive case

Who is she going to the movies *with?* →
With whom is she going to the movies?
С кем она́ идёт в кино́?
object of the preposition **с**,
which here takes the instrumental case

▼▼▼▼▼▼▼▼▼▼▼▼▼▼▼REVIEW ▼▼▼▼▼▼▼▼▼▼▼▼▼▼▼▼

I. Underline the prepositions in the sentences below.

1. Let's not sit at that table by the window.

2. An omlet without eggs? Impossible.

3. If we leave before noon, we'll be in Tula by six.

4. Due to circumstances beyond our control, we will show the movie
   Ivan the Terrible instead of *Alexander I.*

II. Rewrite the sentences below so that the object of the preposition comes
    after the preposition and parallels Russian sentence structure.

1. What are you going to the store for?

_____

2. I don't know what you're talking about.

_____

3. Who's the fight between?

_____

4. Who did you vote in favor of?

_____

30. WHAT IS AN ADVERB?

An **adverb** is a word that modifies or describes a verb, an adjective, or another adverb. Adverbs indicate manner, quantity, time, place, and intensity.

Rostov fights *well.*
|
modifies the verb *fight*

Gogol's characters are *very* complicated.
|
modifies the adjective *complicated*

Natasha fell in love *too easily.*
| |
modifies   modifies
adverb   verb
easily   *fell*

IN ENGLISH

Here are some examples of adverbs:

- adverbs of manner, which are the most common, can be recognized by their *-ly* endings; they answer the question *how?, in what way?*

    Turgenev writes *very precisely.*
    Mr. Karenin spoke *courteously.*

- adverbs of quantity or degree answer the question *how much?* or *to what extent?*

    Ivan Ilych feared death *greatly.*
    Raskolnikov's plan worked *very well.*

- adverbs of time answer the question *when?*

    Anna will come *soon.*
    Her train arrived *late.*

- adverbs of place answer the question *where?*

    Bazarov looked *around.*
    Arkady was left *behind.*

- adverbs of cause or purpose answer the question *why?, what for?*

    Why did he do that?
    I will *therefore* refuse to vote.

- adverbs of intensity are used for emphasis

    Vronsky did not *actually* commit suicide.
    Chekhov is a *really* fine writer.

Many words in English function both as adjectives and adverbs without a change in form to help identify their different roles in a sentence. To avoid confusion, remember that adjectives modify nouns and pronouns, while adverbs modify verbs, adjectives and other adverbs.

Frou-Frou is a *fast* horse.
modifies the noun *horse* → adjective

Frou-Frou ran *fast*.
modifies the verb *ran* → adverb

Vodka is the *only* drink for me.
modifies the noun *drink* → adjective

I *only* drink vodka.
modifies the verb *drink* → adverb

IN RUSSIAN

Adverbs in Russian operate in much the same way as in English. The most important thing to remember about adverbs is that they are invariable; they never change case and they do not have gender or number.

*She writes **well**.*
Она́ **хорошо́** пишет.
  modifies the singular verb *writes*

*They write **well**.*
Они́ **хорошо́** пишут.
  modifies the plural verb *write*

*This is a **well** written report.*
prepositional phrase, prepositional case

Это **хорошо́** напи́санный докла́д.
  modifies adjectival form *written*

It is especially important to distinguish adverbs from adjectives, which do change in gender, number and case, depending upon the nouns they modify.

*We respect **good** people.*
modifies the noun *people* → adjective
Мы уважа́ем **хоро́ших** люде́й.
agrees with *people*
plural number, accusative case

*She writes **well**.*
modifies the verb *writes* → adverb
Она́ **хорошо́** пи́шет.
no gender, no number, no case

*There is a **fast** current here.*
modifies the noun *current* → adjective
Здесь **бы́строе** тече́ние.
agrees with *current*
neut. sing. nominative case

*My car goes **fast**.*
modifies the verb *goes* → adverb
Моя́ маши́на **бы́стро** е́здит.
no gender, no number, no case

▼▼▼▼▼▼▼▼▼▼▼▼▼▼▼▼REVIEW ▼▼▼▼▼▼▼▼▼▼▼▼▼▼▼▼

I. Circle the adverbs in the sentences below.
- Draw an arrow from the adverb to the word it modifies.

1. He drives carefully.

2. These problems are too difficult.

3. Mary is a good student and she speaks Russian well.

4. He rides his bicycle everywhere.

5. They behaved very well.

II. Identify the *italicized* words as adverbs (ADV) or adjectives (ADJ).

1. Your work was *nicely* done.   ADV   ADJ

2. It was very *nice* of her to write.   ADV   ADJ

3. She drives *fast*.   ADV   ADJ

4. The current is *fast*.   ADV   ADJ

5. I heard a *sudden* noise.   ADV   ADJ

6. She *suddenly* died.   ADV   ADJ

7. I saw her *late* in the day.   ADV   ADJ

8. We had a *late* dinner.   ADV   ADJ

31. WHAT IS A CONJUNCTION?

A **conjunction** is a word that links words or groups of words. Like adverbs and prepositions, conjunctions are invariable, that is they **never** change: they do not have number, gender, or case.

IN ENGLISH

There are two kinds of conjunctions: coordinating and subordinating.

Coordinating conjunctions join words, phrases and clauses that are equal; they coordinate elements of equal rank. The major coordinating conjunctions in English are *and, but, or, nor,* and *for.*

> good *or* evil
> over the river *and* through the woods
> They invited us, *but* we couldn't come.

Subordinating conjunctions join a dependent clause to the main clause; they subordinate one thought to another one; that is, they indicate the relationship of unequal elements. A clause introduced by a subordinating conjunction is called a dependent or subordinate clause (see p. 160). Typical subordinating conjunctions are *before, after, since, although, because, if, unless, so that, while, that,* and *whatever.*

main clause

Although we were invited, we didn't go.
  |
subordinating conjunction

main clause

They left *because* they were bored.
  |
subordinating conjunction

main clause

He said *that* he was tired.
  |
subordinating conjunction

Notice that the main clause is not always the first clause of the sentence.

Preposition or Subordinating Conjunction?

Some words function as both prepositions and subordinating conjunctions. We can tell the difference between these "look alike" words by determining if the word introduces a clause. If the word introduces the clause, it is a subordinating conjunction (SC). That clause will contain a subject and a verb (see **What are Sentences, Phrases and Clauses?** p. 158).

We left *after* the intermission began.
| SC   subject + verb

We left *after* he came.
      SC   subject + verb

If the word in question does not introduce a clause, it is a preposition (P). The prepositional phrase contains an object, but no verb.

We left *after* the intermission.
      P   object of preposition

After the concert we ate ice cream.
  P   object of preposition

IN RUSSIAN

Conjunctions in Russian operate in much the same way they do in English. The most common coordinating conjunctions are: **и** *(and),* **а** *(and, but, whereas)* and **но** *(but).* Study your textbook carefully to distinguish between the uses of these words.

Unlike English, Russian conjunctions do not also function as prepositions. An English "look alike" conjunction, which introduces a clause, will always be translated into Russian using a preposition followed by a "filler" word in the case required by the preposition.

*We left **after** the intermission.*
      preposition
Мы ушли **после** перерыва.
        P   object of the preposition

          subordinate clause
*We left **after** she came.*
      conjunction
            subordinate clause
Мы ушли **после того**, как она пришла.
  preposition takes   "filler" word in the genitive case
  genitive case

*I will read **before** supper.*
        |
    preposition

Я бу́ду чита́ть **пе́ред** у́жином.
              | |
          preposition   object of preposition

*I will read it **before** you arrive.*
            |
        conjunction

Я его́ прочита́ю **пе́ред** тем, как ты придёшь.
               | |
        preposition "filler word"

As a beginning student of Russian, you will not study this type of construction, but to avoid making mistakes in the use of prepositions you must be able to recognize whether "look alike" words in English are prepositions or conjunctions.

▼▼▼▼▼▼▼▼▼▼▼▼▼▼▼▼▼**REVIEW** ▼▼▼▼▼▼▼▼▼▼▼▼▼▼▼▼▼▼

Identify the *italicized* words as prepositions (P) or conjunctions (C).

1. We must finish *by* noon.   P   C

2. Speak to her *before* you leave.   P   C

3. Translate *into* Russian.   P   C

4. I've known him *since* he was a child.   P   C

5. He's nice *except* when he's tired.   P   C

32. WHAT IS A RELATIVE PRONOUN?

A **relative pronoun** serves two purposes:

- As a pronoun it stands for a noun or another pronoun previously mentioned called its **antecedent** (see p. 33).

  There is the woman *who* fell under the train.

　　　　　antecedent　　relative pronoun

- It introduces a **subordinate clause**, that is, a group of words having a subject and verb separate from the main clause (see **What are Sentences, Phrases and Clauses?**, p. 158).

  　　　main clause　　　　　subordinate clause

This is the woman *who* fell under the train.

The subordinate clause "who fell under the train" is also called a **relative clause** because it starts with a relative pronoun *(who)*. The relative pronoun *who* refers back the subordinate clause to its antecedent, *woman*.

Sometimes the placement of the subordinate (or relative) clause in the sentence will divide the main clause into two parts:

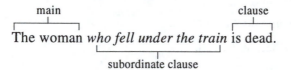

In English and in Russian the choice of the relative pronoun will depend upon its function in the relative clause. You must train yourself to go through the following steps:

1. CLAUSE—Find the relative clause.

2. FUNCTION—Determine the function of the relative pronoun in the relative clause.

   - Is it the subject?
   - Is it the direct object?
   - Is it the indirect object?
   - Is it an object of a preposition?
   - Is it a possessive modifier?

3. PERSON OR THING—Select the proper relative pronoun based on the antecedent.

- Is it a person?
- Is it a thing?

IN ENGLISH

Relative pronouns include *who, which,* and *that.* Their forms change according to their function in the relative clause and their antecedent in the main clause.

Only the relative pronoun for persons shows different case forms in English: *who* (subjective), *whom* (objective), and *whose* (possessive). The relative pronouns *which* and *that* do not change form for different cases.

We will study *who, which* and *that* used as relative pronouns in turn. Keep in mind, however, that sometimes more than one pronoun may be used in a given sentence. Whatever relative pronoun is used, its form is always determined by the antecedent and by its function in the relative clause.

Who, whose and ***whom*** refer to people.

relative clause

He *who* hesitates falls on his face.

subject of relative clause

pronoun antecedent

relative clause

I don't know *whose* book this is.

possessive modifier

> Note: The antecedent of *whose* is not specifically indicated in the sentence, but *whose* can refer to a single person or to many. *Whose* may also be synonymous with *"of which"* and refer to things. See p. 108.

relative clause

The man *whom* Bazarov wounded is recuperating.

antecedent   object of relative clause

relative clause

The woman with *whom* you spoke is a double agent.

antecedent   object of a preposition *with*

Which refers to animals and things and to groups of people when they are described with a singular word.

relative clause

This is the horse *which* Napoleon rode.

antecedent object of the relative clause

relative clause

The candle by *which* she read blew out.

antecedent   object of the preposition *by* in relative clause

Kutuzov's army, *which* camped here, was exhausted.

subject of the relative clause

antecedent, sing. group of people

When *which* is used as a possessive *(of which)*, it is often replaced by *whose*. The two sentences below are the same in meaning; *of which* and *whose* have the same antecedent.

relative clause

The novel, the chapters *of which* are in verse, is by Pushkin.

antecedent   object of the preposition *of* in relative clause

relative clause

The novel, *whose* chapters are in verse, is by Pushkin.

antecedent possessive modifier *"of which"*

Do not confuse *whose* referring to inanimate objects (in the example above) with *whose* referring to animate beings (see under 1 above).

That refers to people, animals and things. *That* is the most commonly used relative pronoun and may substitute for *who* or *which* except after a preposition.

relative clause

Here is the man *that* wants to see you.

antecedent   subject of relative clause may be replaced by *who* relative clause

Here is the man about *whom* I spoke.

antecedent   relative pronoun object of preposition *about*

Careful

1. Recognize the difference between *that* used as a relative pronoun and *that* used as a conjunction (see **What is a Conjunction?**, p. 103).

   ▪ relative pronoun: always follows a noun, its antecedent.

   antecedent noun

   I know the boy *that* is coming.

   relative pronoun (may be substituted by *who)*

   ▪ conjunction: connects two independent clauses

   clause   clause

   I know *that* he is coming.

   conjunction joining two independent clauses

   A different Russian word is used for *that,* depending upon its part of speech.

2. Recognize the difference between *who, which* or *whose* used as a relative pronoun and *who, which* or *whose* used as an interrogative pronoun (see **What is an Interrogative Pronoun?,** p. 54).

   ▪ relative pronoun: always follows a noun, its antecedent

   antecedent noun

   The masked man *who* rode off left a silver bullet.

   relative pronoun

   ▪ interrogative pronoun: related to a question

   Who was that masked man?

   interrogative pronoun

   Which was the witch *which* watched the watch?

   interrogative pronoun   relative pronoun

   A different Russian word is used depending on the part of speech.

3. In colloquial English you will often hear sentences in which the preposition *which* introduces the relative clause comes at the end of the sentence, separated from its object. When a preposition is separated from its object it is called a **dangling preposition**.

> Here is the book *which* you were talking *about*.
>   relative pronoun   preposition

Before you translate a sentence of this type into Russian you should rearrange the word order so that the preposition stands in front of its object. This will help you to identify the relative clause.

>   relative clause
> Here is the book *about which* you are talking.

4. Colloquial English sometimes uses the subject pronoun *who* as an object. It is very important that you know which is the correct form because in Russian *who,* the subjective form, and *whom,* the objective form, are two different words that are not interchangeable.

> We know the woman *who* you like.→
> We know the woman *whom* you like.

The use of *who,* and not *whom,* as the object in a relative clause is especially common when the relative pronoun is used as the object of a preposition.

> The man *who* you spoke *with* is a spy. →
> The man *with whom* you spoke is a spy.

5. Relative pronouns are often omitted in English. Because the relative pronoun must always be expressed in Russian, its function in an English sentence needs to be recognized even if the word is omitted.

> This is the house Jack built. →
> This is the house *that* Jack built.

> Here is the man I met. →
> Here is the man *whom* I met.

IN RUSSIAN

The principal relative pronouns are кото́рый *(who, which* or *that)*; кто *(who)*; что *(what)*; and чей, the possessive modifier of *who (whose).* Study the declension of these pronouns in your textbook.

A relative pronoun usually agrees in gender and number with its antecedent; its case is determined by its function in the relative clause. The relative clause is always set off by commas.

To determine the form of the relative pronoun, here is a series of steps to follow:

1. CHANGES AND CORRECTIONS—Find the relative clause in the English sentence and, if necessary make the following corrections:

   - add the omitted relative pronoun;

   - correct the word order so that the preposition stands before its object and introduces the relative clause; and

   - correct the case of the pronoun.

2. ANTECEDENT—Find the antecedent, if it is stated, and determine which relative pronoun to use.

▪ antecedent stated noun	→	**который**
▪ antecedent animate pronoun or an unstated person	→	**кто**
▪ antecedent inanimate pronoun or an unstated idea	→	**что**
▪ antecedent stated or unstated person, possession indicated	→	**чей**

3. GENDER AND NUMBER—If necessary, determine the gender and number of the antecedent.

4. FUNCTION—Determine the function of the relative pronoun and its corresponding case.

5. SELECTION—Select the form of the pronoun which corresponds to the gender, number and case determined in steps 1-4.

Let us apply these steps to some sample sentences.

I know the girl reading the book.
1. CHANGES AND CORRECTIONS:
omitted relative pronoun *who* added

*I know the girl **who** is reading the book.*
2. ANTECEDENT: *girl,* **девушка,** is a noun. Use **который.**
3. GENDER/NUMBER: **девушка** is fem. sing.
4. FUNCTION/CASE: *who* is the subject of the verb in the relative clause → nominative case

Я знáю дéвушку, **котóрая** читáет кнѝгу.

The apartment I live in is very small.
  1. CHANGES AND CORRECTIONS:
     ▪ omitted relative pronoun *which* added
     ▪ dangling preposition *in* corrected
*The apartment **in which** I live is very small.*
  2. ANTECEDENT: *apartment,* **кварти́ра** is a noun. Use **кото́рый.**
  3. GENDER/NUMBER: **кварти́ра** is fem. sing.
  4. FUNCTION/CASE: *which* is the object of the preposition **в** *(in),* which
     here takes the prepositional case.
Кварти́ра, в **кото́рой** я живу́, о́чень ма́ленькая.

*I know the pianist **who** you wrote to.*
  1. CHANGES AND CORRECTIONS:
     ▪ dangling preposition *to* corrected
     ▪ case of the relative pronoun *who* corrected
*I know the pianist **to whom** you wrote.*
  2. ANTECEDENT: *pianist,* **пиани́ст,** is a noun. Use **кото́рый.**
  3. GENDER/NUMBER: **пиани́ст** is masc. sing.
  4. FUNCTION/CASE: *whom* is the indirect object of the verb of the
     relative clause → dative case
Я зна́ю пиани́ста, **кото́рому** ты писа́ла.

He repeats everything I do.
  1. CHANGES AND CORRECTIONS:
     ▪ omitted relative pronoun *that* added
*He repeats everything **that** I do.*
  2. ANTECEDENT: *everything,* **всё,** is an inanimate pronoun. Use **что.**
  3. GENDER/NUMBER: **что** is always neut. sing.
  4. FUNCTION/CASE: *that* is the direct object of the verb of the
     relative clause → accusative case
Он повторя́ет всё, **что** я де́лаю.

*I don't know **who** she left with.*
  1. CHANGES AND CORRECTIONS:
     ▪ dangling preposition *with* corrected
     ▪ case of the relative pronoun *who* corrected
*I don't know **with whom** she left.*
  2. ANTECEDENT: an unstated person. Use **кто.**
  3. GENDER/NUMBER: **кто** is always masc. sing.
  4. FUNCTION/CASE: *who* is the object of the preposition *(with),*
     which here takes the instrumental case.
Я не зна́ю, с **кем** она́ ушла́.

*I don't know **whose** book she is reading.*
1. CHANGES AND CORRECTIONS: none
2. ANTECEDENT: an unstated person. Possession indicated. Use **чей.**
3. GENDER/NUMBER: **чей** modifies *book,* **кни́га,** a fem. sing. noun
4. FUNCTION/CASE: *whose* modifies a direct object → accusative case

Я не зна́ю, **чью** кни́гу она́ чита́ет.

▼▼▼▼▼▼▼▼▼▼▼▼▼▼REVIEW ▼▼▼▼▼▼▼▼▼▼▼▼▼▼▼▼

Unlike English, the relative pronoun in Russian cannot be omitted.

I. Rewrite the sentences below to include the relative pronoun which must always be expressed in Russian.

1. This is the car I plan to buy.

2. I saw the film you liked.

3. The car I like is too expensive.

II. Rewrite each sentence below by adding the omitted relative pronoun and correcting the word order so that the preposition stands before its object and introduces the relative clause.

1. Who was that masked man you were talking to?

2. What's the name of that restaurant you're always talking about?

3. Where's the new teacher I saw you with?

III. Circle the relative pronouns in the sentences below.

1. Raskolnikov knew that Sonia loved him.

2. Do you know that man?

3. There is the same man that I saw yesterday.

4. Where is the young woman who speaks Ukrainian?

5. Who here speaks Ukrainian?

6. Which horse should I buy?

7. The horse which you showed me is beautiful.

8 . Do you know that I can't swim?

9. Take the book that she is offering you.

10. Take that book.

IV. In the sentences below underline the relative pronoun.
▪ Circle the antecedent.
▪ Identify the function of the relative pronoun. Is it a subject (S), direct object (DO), object of a preposition (OP), or possessive modifier (PM)?

1. I received the letter that you sent me.	S	DO	OP	PM
2. That is the woman who speaks Russian.	S	DO	OP	PM
3. Here comes the man to whom I lent the money.	S	DO	OP	PM
4. This is the desk at which he wrote.	S	DO	OP	PM

33. WHAT IS A REFLEXIVE PRONOUN?

A **reflexive pronoun** is a word used in place of a noun to refer back to or *reflect* the subject of a sentence; it is used either as the object of a verb or as the object of a preposition.

IN ENGLISH

Reflexive pronouns are formed by adding *-self* in the singular and *-selves* in the plural to 1st and 2nd person possessive adjectives (see **What is a Possessive Adjective?,** p. 65) and to 3rd person personal pronouns in the objective case (see p. 40).

Person	Singular	Plural
1st	myself	ourselves
2nd	yourself	yourselves
3rd	himself	
	herself	themselves
	itself	

The reflexive pronoun shows person (1st, 2nd and 3rd) and number (singular or plural) in all forms and gender in the 3rd person singular *(him, her* or *it)*.

Here are some examples of the reflexive pronoun:

- as the object of a verb (see p. 76)

> I cut *myself* with an axe.
> subject direct object
>> *I* is the 1st person singular subject of the verb *cut; myself* is the 1st person singular reflexive pronoun of *I* and is the direct object of the verb.

> *You* should write *yourself* a note.
> subject   indirect object
>> *You* is the 2nd person subject of the verb *should write; yourself* is the 2nd person singular reflexive pronoun of *you* and is the indirect object of the verb.

- as the object of a preposition (see p. 93)

> *He* thinks only of *himself.*
> subject   object of preposition
>> *He* is the 3rd person masculine singular subject of the verb *thinks; himself* is the 3rd person masculine singular reflexive pronoun of *he* and is the object of the preposition *of.*

IN RUSSIAN

The reflexive pronoun **себя**[1] changes case, but it does not show gender, number or person. The reflexive pronoun will translate as *myself, yourself, himself, herself, itself, yourselves,* or *themselves,* depending upon the gender, number and person of the subject to which it refers.

Look at the use of **себя** in the examples below. Observe that in English you do not need to look at the subject to learn the person, gender and number of the reflexive pronoun. In Russian, however, the meaning of the reflexive pronoun comes from the subject of the sentence.

- as the direct object of a verb

> *She saw **herself** in the mirror.*
>   3rd pers. fem. sing.
> **Она́** ви́дела **себя́** в зе́ркале.
> subject   direct object
> 3rd pers. sing. accusative case

> *Are **you** behaving **yourselves** well?*
>   2nd pers. pl.
> **Вы** хорошо́ **себя́** ведёте?
> subject   direct object
> 2nd pers. pl. accusative case

- as the indirect object of a verb

> *I bought **myself** ice cream.*
>   1st pers. sing.
> **Я** купи́ла **себе́** моро́женое.
> subject   indirect object
> 1st pers. sing. dative case

---

[1]Since a reflexive pronoun cannot be the subject of a sentence, it does not have a nominative case , which is the form by which words that decline are called and listed in the dictionary. It is named by its genitive/accusative case form.

- as the object of a preposition

> **They** *don't think about* **themselves.**
> |
> 3rd pers. pl.

Они не ду́мают о **себе́.**
| |
subject   object of the preposition o
3rd pers. pl.   prepositional case

▼▼▼▼▼▼▼▼▼▼▼▼▼▼▼REVIEW ▼▼▼▼▼▼▼▼▼▼▼▼▼▼▼▼▼

Fill in the proper reflexive pronoun.

1. I bought _____ a new car.

2. Don't try to lift that by _____.

3. We wish we could give _____ a long vacation.

4. Mary always blames _____.

5. Mary, don't be so hard on _____.

6. He doesn't know what to do with _____.

34. WHAT IS AN INTENSIVE PRONOUN?

An **intensive pronoun** (sometimes called an **emphatic pronoun**) is a word used to strengthen and emphasize a noun or pronoun. The intensive pronoun is placed right after the noun or other pronoun to which it refers.

An intensive pronoun cannot stand by itself; it must always be linked to another word, the word which it emphasizes and intensifies. These two words are said to be in **apposition**.

IN ENGLISH

Intensive pronouns are identical in form to reflexive pronouns; you can tell these pronouns apart by contrasting their different functions.

Compare:

She *herself* is to blame.

intensive pronoun
in apposition to *she*

She blamed *herself.*

reflexive pronoun
direct object

I did this for the director *himself.*

intensive pronoun
in apposition to *director*

I did this for *myself.*

reflexive pronoun
object of the preposition *for*

IN RUSSIAN

The intensive pronoun **сам** agrees in person, gender, number and case with the word to which it is in apposition.

*She **herself** is to blame.*
Она **сама́** винова́та.

fem. sing. nominative case intensive pronoun
in apposition to **она́,** fem. sing. nominative case

*I said this to the director **himself**.*
Я э́то сказа́ла **самому́** дире́ктору.

masc. sing. dative case intensive pronoun
in apposition to **дире́ктору,** masc. sing. dative case

▼▼▼▼▼▼▼▼▼▼▼▼▼▼▼▼▼REVIEW ▼▼▼▼▼▼▼▼▼▼▼▼▼▼▼▼▼

[on reflexive and intensive pronouns]

Identify the pronouns in the sentences below as reflexive pronouns (RP) or intensive pronouns (IP).

- Draw an arrow to the noun or pronoun to which each reflexive or intensive pronoun refers.

	RP	IP
1. Did you buy yourselves tickets?	RP	IP
2. Did you buy the tickets yourself?	RP	IP
3. The director himself spoke.	RP	IP
4. We spoke to the director herself.	RP	IP
5. Lena, behave yourself.	RP	IP
6. Did Vanya himself come to the office?	RP	IP
7. They themselves are to blame.	RP	IP
8. We blamed ourselves.	RP	IP
9. Know yourself.	RP	IP
10. You should know the answer yourself.	RP	IP

35. WHAT ARE INDEFINITE AND NEGATIVE PRONOUNS AND ADVERBS?

An **indefinite pronoun** is a word used to refer to an unidentified person or thing. The word *indefinite* means "not definite," "undefined" *(someone, anything)*.

An **indefinite adverb** is a word used to refer to the place, time, or purpose of an action when the speaker does not have a complete or clear idea of the action or does not wish to be specific *(somewhere, anyhow)*.

A **negative pronoun** is the negative equivalent of an indefinite pronoun; it *negates* or denies the existence of someone or something *(nobody, nothing)*.

A **negative adverb** is the negative equivalent of an indefinite adverb; it negates or denies the place, time, or purpose of an action *(nowhere, never)*.

Indefinite and Negative Pronouns

IN ENGLISH

Because each indefinite pronoun has a corresponding negative pronoun, it is helpful to study these pronouns as pairs. The most common pairs are:

Indefinite	Negative
someone	no one
anyone	
somebody	nobody
anybody	
something	nothing
anything	

Negative pronouns enable us to respond negatively to questions which contain an indefinite pronoun.

Is *anyone* coming? *Nobody.*
indefinite pronoun   negative pronoun

Is *something* wrong? *Nothing.*
indefinite pronoun   negative pronoun

The above examples are one-word answers. If we answer negatively with a complete sentence, we have to respect the strict rule which says that there can only be one negative word in any one clause (see **What are Sentences, Phrases and Clauses?, p. 158**).

Here are some examples showing how we apply this rule when answering different types of questions.

- a question with one indefinite pronoun

    Did he say *anything?*

A negative answer to this question may negate either the verb or the indefinite pronoun (but not both). It is more common to negate the verb.

                       verb negated

answer 1   He did*n't* say *anything.*

                                    indefinite pronoun
                                    no change

                 verb no change

answer 2   He said *nothing.*

                  indefinite pronoun negated
                  negative pronoun

- a question with two indefinite pronouns

    Does *anyone* know *anything* about that?

The verb is never negated in a sentence with more than one indefinite word and only one of the two indefinite pronouns is negated. The other one does not change.

           verb   indefinite pronoun
        no change   no change

No one knows *anything* about that.

indefinite pronoun negated
negative pronoun

In children's speech we often hear incorrect use of more than one negative in a clause. This mistake is called a **double negative.** Correct speech requires that all but one negative word (usually the negated verb) be replaced by indefinite words.

incorrect I did*n't* see *nobody.*
correct   I did*n't* see *anybody.*

| **incorrect** | I do*n't* want to play with *nobody.* |
| **correct** | I do*n't* want to play with *anybody.* |

IN RUSSIAN

Indefinite pronouns are formed by attaching the suffixes **-то** or **-нибудь** to interrogative pronouns:

кто́-**то**	*somebody, someone*
что́-**то**	*something*
кто́-**нибудь**	*anybody, anyone*
что́-**нибудь**	*anything*

These forms are not always equivalent in meaning to their English counterparts. Be sure to study your textbook carefully to learn the differences.

Negative pronouns are formed by adding the prefix **ни-** to interrogative pronouns.

| **никто́** | *nobody, no one* |
| **ничто́** | *nothing* |

As opposed to English, which permits only one negative word to a clause, Russian sentences can have an unlimited number of negatives. Regardless of the number of **ни-** words, any verb in the sentence must be negated with the negative particle **не** *(not).*

*I didn't give **anything** to anyone.*
Я **ни**кому́ **ни**чего́ **не** дава́л.

*I don't know **anyone.***
Я **ни**кого́ **не** зна́ю.

***Nobody** knows **anything** about that.*
Никто́ **ни**чего́ **не** зна́ет об э́том.

Indefinite and Negative Adverbs

IN ENGLISH

What we have said about the use of indefinite and negative pronouns also applies to indefinite and negative adverbs (see **What is an Adverb?**, p. 99).

Here are some common indefinite and negative adverbs:

Indefinite	Negative
somewhere	nowhere
anywhere	
ever	never

Negative adverbs enable us to respond negatively to questions which contain an indefinite adverb.

Do you *ever* agree? *Never.*
        | |
    indefinite   negative
    adverb   adverb

Are you going *somewhere? Nowhere.*
                | |
        indefinite   negative
        adverb   adverb

The above examples are one-word answers. If we answer negatively with a complete sentence, we have to respect the strict rule which says that there can only be one negative word in any one clause. Here are some examples showing how we apply this rule when answering different types of questions.

▪ a question with one indefinite adverb

Does he go *anywhere?*

A negative answer to this question may negate either the verb or the indefinite adverb, but not both. It is more common to negate the verb.

verb negated
    |
He does*n't* go *anywhere.*
               |
           indefinite adverb
           no change

verb no change
    |
He goes *nowhere.*
         |
      indefinite adverb negated
      negative adverb

▪ a question with two indefinite adverbs

Does she *ever* go *anywhere?*

The verb is never negated in a sentence with more than one indefinite word and only one of the two indefinite adverbs is negated. The other one does not change.

            verb   indefinite adverb
          no change   no change
           | |
She *never* goes *anywhere.*
    |
indefinite adverb negated
negative adverb

IN RUSSIAN

What we have said about the formation and use of indefinite and negative pronouns in Russian also applies to indefinite and negative adverbs.

Here are some common indefinite and negative adverbs:

Indefinite		Negative	
куда́-то	*somewhere*	никуда́	*nowhere*
куда́-нибудь	*anywhere*		
когда́-то	*ever, (once)*	никогда́	*never*
когда́-нибудь	*ever, some day*		

Just as we have explained in the discussion of negative pronouns above, Russian sentences with negative adverbs can have an unlimited number of negatives. Regardless of the number of **ни-** words, any verb in the sentence must be negated with the negative particle **не**.

Are you going anywhere this summer?
Вы куда́-нибудь е́дете э́тим ле́том.

*No, I'm **not** going **anywhere**.*
Нет, я **никуда́ не** е́ду.

*I **never** go **anywhere** in the summer.*
Я **никогда́ никуда́ не** е́зжу ле́том.

Hidden Negatives

IN ENGLISH

When there is more than one indefinite word in the sentence the verb is never negated and only one of the two indefinite words is negated.

Will you *ever* say *something* in Russian?

    verb   indefinite pronoun
    no change   no change

I will *never* say *anything* in Russian.

indefinite adverb negated
negative adverb

IN RUSSIAN

While in English there can only one negative word in a sentence, in Russian, as we have already stated, all the indefinite words and the verb are negated. In the examples below, a line is drawn to connect the Russian word with its English counterpart.

*I will **never** want to eat **anything** again.*
Я бо́льше **никогда́ ничего́ не** захочу́ есть.
　　　　　　never　　　nothing not

Nobody ever talked with anyone about anything.
Никто́ никогда́ ни с ке́м[1] **ни о чём не** говори́л.
　nobody　never　　no one　　　nothing　not

Working from Russian to English in sentences of this type does not normally create any problems for students of Russian. We have been drilled in childhood to avoid double negatives.

When you translate from English into Russian, however, you must be able to recognize and add the "hidden" negatives, that is, words that are not expressed negatively in English, but must be expressed with negatives in Russian.

Here are a series of steps to follow when you are working from English to Russian:

1. NEGATIVE WORD—Is there a negative word in the sentence? If so, go on.

2. INDEFINITE WORD—Are there any indefinite words in the sentence? If so, go on.

3. REPLACEMENT—Replace the indefinite words with their negative counterparts.

4. VERB—Negate the verb.

5. TRANSLATE—Translate into Russian using a negative word for every negative you have created in steps 3 and 4.

> *I will **never** want to eat **anything** again.*
> 　1. NEGATIVE WORD: *never*
> 　2. INDEFINITE WORD: *anything*
> 　3. REPLACEMENT: *anything → nothing*
> 　4. VERB: *eat→not* eat
> Я бо́льше **никогда́ ничего́ не** захочу́ есть.

> *Nobody ever talked with anyone about anything.*
> 　1. NEGATIVE WORD: *nobody*
> 　2. INDEFINITE WORD: *ever, anything, anyone*
> 　3. REPLACEMENT: *ever→never, anyone→no one, anything→nothing*
> 　4. VERB: *talked→* did *not* talk
> **Никто́ никогда́ ни с ке́м**[1] **ни о чём**[1] **не** говори́л.

---

[1] When a negative pronoun is the object of a preposition the preposition is placed between the **ни** and the pronoun, thereby creating three separate words.

▼▼▼▼▼▼▼▼▼▼▼▼▼▼▼REVIEW ▼▼▼▼▼▼▼▼▼▼▼▼▼▼▼▼▼

I. In the space provided give the negative forms for the following indefinite pronouns and adverbs.

1. ever _____

2. anyone _____

3. anything _____

4. anybody _____

5. something _____

6. anywhere _____

7. somewhere _____

II. In the sentences below underline all the indefinite and negative pronouns and adverbs. Rewrite the sentences changing these indefinite forms to their negative counterparts, which is what you would need to do to express the sentence in Russian.

1. I have never seen anyone anywhere with such a long nose.

_____

2. Nobody said anything about anybody.

_____

3. I never go anywhere alone.

_____

36. WHAT IS MEANT BY COMPARISON OF ADJECTIVES?

When adjectives are used to compare qualities of the nouns they modify they change forms. This change is called **comparison.**

comparison of adjectives

The moon is *bright,* but the sun is *brighter.*

adjective modifying   adjective modifying
the noun *moon*   the noun *sun*

There are three degrees of comparison: positive, comparative, superlative.

IN ENGLISH

Let us go over what is meant by the different degrees of comparison and how each degree is formed.

The **positive** degree refers to the quality of one person or thing. It is simply the adjectival form.

> The professor is *wise.*
> The moon is *bright.*
> This horse is *beautiful.*

The **comparative** degree compares two objects, persons or qualities.

- The simple comparative is formed by adding -*er* to the positive degree of generally short adjectives.

> This professor is *wiser* than most.
> The sun is *brighter* than the moon.

- The compound comparative is formed by adding *more* or *less* before the positive degree of longer adjectives.

> This horse is *more* beautiful.
> Ivan's speech is *more* interesting.

The **superlative** degree is used to compare three or more items or to stress the highest degree of quality. It is formed:

- by adding -*est* to the positive degree of short adjectives

> This professor is the *wisest* woman I know.
> This student is the *brightest* one in her class.

- by placing *the most* or *very* in front of the positive form of longer adjectives

> This horse is *the most* beautiful of all.
> Solzhenitsyn's speech was *very* interesting.

IN RUSSIAN

Comparative adjectives have the same degrees as in English: positive, comparative, superlative.

1. The **positive** degree of the adjective is the dictionary form of the adjective. The positive degree adjective always agrees in gender, number and case with the noun it modifies (see **What is a Descriptive Adjective,** p. 61).

но́вый дом	*a **new** house*
молода́я ло́шадь	*a **young** horse*

2. The **comparative** degree of the adjective has two forms: one that is invariable and one that declines to agree with the noun or pronoun that it modifies. The formation of the comparative is complex, refer to the textbook.

Simple comparative (composed of one word) adjectives are invariable; they do not change in gender, number or case. Their use is required if the adjective is a predicate adjective (see p. 30).

My students are *younger* than Asya.

                         |

                predicate adjective
Мои́ студе́нты **моло́же** Аси.

Horses are *smarter* than you think.

                     |

                predicate adjective
Ло́шади **умне́е**, чем ты ду́маешь.

Compound comparative (composed of two words) adjectives are used attributively, that is, they come before a noun or pronoun. These forms consist of an invariable **бо́лее** *(more)* or **ме́нее** *(less)* and the positive degree of the adjective, which agrees in case, number and gender with the word it modifies.

*Today she gave a **more interesting** lecture.*

                          |

             modifies *lecture,* the direct object
Она́ сего́дня чита́ла **бо́лее интере́сную** ле́кцию.

                                    |

                      compound comparative adjective

                      modifies **ле́кция,** fem. sing. noun,

                      direct object in the accusative case

*He is a **less interesting** person.*

              |

     modifies *person,* the predicate noun
Он **ме́нее интере́сный** челове́к.

            |

     compound comparative adjective

     modifies **челове́к,** masc. sing. noun,

     predicate noun in the nominative case

3. The **superlative** degree of adjectives also has two forms. Both forms agree in gender, number and case with the noun they modify.

Simple superlative adjectives emphasize a very high degree of quality. They are formed by adding **-ейший** or **-айший** to the stem of the positive degree adjective and they agree in gender, number and case with the noun they modify. These forms are uncommon in conversational Russian.

*She told me about an **extremely interesting** person.*

> modifies *person*
> object of the preposition *about*

Она́ мне рассказа́ла об **интере́снейшем** челове́ке.

> simple superlative adjective
> modifies **челове́к,** masc. sing. noun
> object of the preposition **об** *(about),*
> which takes the prepositional case

Compound superlative adjectives are formed by adding the adjective **са́мый** before the positive degree of the adjective. Both words agree in gender, number and case with the word they modify. These forms are very common in conversational Russian.

*She is the **smartest** student in the freshman class.*

> modifies *student,* the predicate noun

Она́ **са́мая у́мная** студе́нтка на пе́рвом ку́рсе.

> compound superlative adjective
> modifies **студе́нтка,** a fem. sing. noun
> predicate in the nominative case

*The **largest** city in the Russia is Moscow.*

> modifies *city,* the subject

Са́мый большо́й го́род в Росси́и—э́то Москва́.

> compound superlative adjective
> modifies **го́род,** masc. sing. noun
> subject in the nominative case

▼▼▼▼▼▼▼▼▼▼▼▼▼▼▼▼REVIEW ▼▼▼▼▼▼▼▼▼▼▼▼▼▼▼▼▼

I. In the sentences below circle the adjectives and mark them as positive (P), comparative (C), or superlative (S) degree.

1. He is boring.   P   C   S

2. She is a most energetic student.   P   C   S

3. I have rarely seen a better film.   P   C   S

4. Mark is my best friend.   P   C   S

5. Your answer is less convincing.   P   C   S

6. December is the busiest month.   P   C   S

7. January is also a busy month.   P   C   S

II. Underline the comparative adjectives in the sentences. Identify which are attributive (AA) and which are predicate adjectives (PA).

1. I want to buy a cheaper house.   AA   PA

2. He is taller than I am.   AA   PA

3. She is a more popular teacher.   AA   PA

4. This novel is shorter.   AA   PA

5. This is a shorter novel.   AA   PA

6. This house is cheaper.   AA   PA

37. WHAT IS MEANT BY ACTIVE AND PASSIVE VOICE?

The **voice** of the verb refers to the relationship between the verb and its subject. There are two voices:

A sentence is said to be in the **active voice** when the verb expresses what the subject of the verb is or does, i.e., the subject of the sentence is the "doer" of the action. In this instance the verb is called an **active verb.**

> The Russians burned Moscow.

The active verb helps to express an idea vigorously and concisely and is most often heard in conversational speech. The majority of active verbs are transitive, that is, they take a direct object.

> The Russians burned Moscow.
>   subject   verb   direct object

A sentence is said to be in the **passive voice** when the verb expresses what is done to the subject by someone or something. In this instance the verb is called a **passive verb.**

> Moscow *was burned.*
>   subject   passive verb

If the doer of the action is stated it is called the **agent.**

> Moscow *was burned* by the Russians.
>   subject   verb   agent

In rewriting a sentence from an active to a passive construction, the direct object becomes the subject and the subject becomes the agent.

> **active**   The Russians *burned* Moscow.
>   subject active verb direct object
>
> **passive**   Moscow *was burned* by the Russians.
>   subject   verb   agent

Passive constructions are most commonly used in formal written language.

IN ENGLISH

The passive voice is expressed by the conjugated verb *to be* + the past participle of the main verb (see **What is a Participle?,** p. 145). The tense of the verb *to be* indicates the tense of the passive construction. In conversational English the agent is rarely expressed.

	Active	Passive
present	it burns	it is burned
past	it burned	it was burned
future	it will burn	it will be burned

active

They *are building* a school.

$\quad$ subject $\quad$ verb $\quad$ direct object
$\qquad\qquad$ present

↓

passive

A school *is being built* (by them).

$\quad$ subject $\qquad$ verb $\qquad$ agent
$\qquad\qquad$ passive present

active

Vronsky *will race* the horse.

$\quad$ subject $\quad$ verb $\quad$ direct object
$\qquad\qquad$ future

↓

passive

The horse *will be raced* (by Vronsky).

$\quad$ subject $\qquad$ verb $\qquad$ agent
$\qquad\qquad$ passive future

IN RUSSIAN

The only true opposition of active and passive voice occurs in participles. Before you read further be sure to consult **What is a Participle?**, p. 145. The passive voice is expressed by the verb *to be* + the short-form passive participle of the main verb. As in English, the tense of the verb *to be* indicates the tense of the passive construction.

present	Это написано.
	It is written.
past	Это **было** написано.
	It was written.
future	Это **будет** написано.
	It will be written.

All short-form passive participles behave like predicate adjectives (see **What is a Predicate?**, p. 30), that is, they agree with the noun they modify (in this case the subject) in gender and number. They do not decline.

The letter is well written.
Письмо́ хорошо́ напи́сано.

neut. sing.   neut. sing.
subject   present tense
                short-form passive participle

The book will be written.
Кни́га бу́дет напи́сана.

fem. sing.   fem. sing.
subject   future tense
                short-form passive participle

In conversational Russian you will rarely hear short-form passive constructions with an agent. If the agent of the action is expressed it is always in the instrumental case.

The letter was written by Tatiana.
Письмо́ бы́ло напи́сано Татья́ной.

neut. sing.   agent of the action
subject   neuter sing.   instrumental case
          past tense
          short-form
          passive participle

These poems were written by my friend.
Эти стихи́ бы́ли напи́саны мои́м дру́гом.

neut. pl.   plural   agent of the action
subject   past tense   instrumental case
        short-form
        passive participle

Careful

With the exception of the short-form passive participle discussed above you will not often see the passive voice in spoken Russian. Russian avoids passive constructions.

1. English passive constructions which express a general statement may be translated with the help of the particle -ся (see p. 76) added to an active voice verb:

   How is this word written?
   Как пи́шется э́то сло́во?

   Ten is divided (is divisible) by two.
   Де́сять де́лится на два.

   This city is called St.Petersburg.
   Этот го́род называ́ется Санкт Петербу́рг.

2. English passive constructions without a stated agent may be translated by a 3rd person plural active verb without a stated subject. The subject in English becomes the direct object in Russian.

> *A school is being built.*
> *(They) are building a school.*
> Стро́ят шко́лу.

> *What is written in the paper?*
> *What do (they) write in the paper?*
> Что пи́шут в газе́те?

> *Are you understood when you speak Russian?*
> *Do (they) understand you when you speak Russian?*
> Вас понима́ют, когда́ вы говори́те по-ру́сски?

▼▼▼▼▼▼▼▼▼▼▼▼▼▼REVIEW ▼▼▼▼▼▼▼▼▼▼▼▼▼▼▼▼

I. The following sentences are in the passive voice. The agent is in *italics*. Rewrite the sentences into the active voice changing the agent into the subject.

1. The books were returned *by me*.

_____

2. The game was won *by the Spartak team*.

_____

3. The letter was written *by your friend*.

_____

II. The following sentences are in the active voice. The subject is in *italics*. Rewrite the sentences into the passive voice changing the subject into the agent.

1. *I* wrote the book.

_____

2. Will *you* mow the lawn?

_____

3. The *producer* gave them free tickets.

_____

III. Identify the voice of the verb as active (A) or passive (P).

1. The store will be opened at nine.	A	P
2. Mary usually opens the store.	A	P
3. The new barn was built last year.	A	P
4. When did they finish building the barn?	A	P
5. The noise awakened me.	A	P
6. I was awakened at midnight.	A	P

38. WHAT IS MEANT BY MOOD?

Verbs have **mood**, that is, they indicate the speakers' attitude toward what they are saying. The word "mood" is a variation of the word *mode,* meaning manner or way.

IN ENGLISH

Verbs can be in one of three moods:

1. The **indicative mood** is used to express or indicate facts. This is the most common mood, and most verbs that you use in everyday conversation belong to the indicative mood. It is the only mood which indicates time.

present	Russian bread *is* very tasty.
past	I *paid* 15 kopecks for the bread.
future	*Will* you ever *eat* Russian bread?

    (See **What is the Present Tense?**, p. 82; **What is the Past Tense?**, p. 85; **What is the Future Tense?**, p. 89.)

2. The **imperative mood** expresses a command, that is, gives an order (see **What is the Imperative?**, p. 137).

    Don't drink the water!
    Let them eat artichokes!
    Row, row, row your boat!

3. The **subjunctive mood** expresses an action that is not real. It is the language of wish, possibility, doubt and hypothetical condition (see **What are the Subjunctive and Conditional?**, p. 141).

    I wish *I were* vacationing on the Black Sea.
    I would visit Moscow if I had the money.
    If I were rich *I would own* horses.

IN RUSSIAN

As in English verbs can be divided into three moods:

The indicative and imperative moods correspond in English and Russian.

The subjunctive mood, however, does not exist in Russian. Many of its uses, however, are expressed by the conditional mood (see **What are the Subjunctive and Conditional?**, p. 141).

39. WHAT IS THE IMPERATIVE?

The **imperative** is the command form of the verb. It is used to give an order.

IN ENGLISH

There are three types of commands, each using the dictionary form or "bare" infinitive of the verb (see p. 71).

"You" **command**—The **"you"** or **second-person command** is used when giving a direct order to one or many persons. The subject pronoun "you," either singular or plural, is not stated in the command.

> *Don't smoke!*
> *Go away!*
> Please *think* about this.

"First-person" **command**—The **first-person** or **inclusive command** is more of an invitation, given to oneself or to others. It is used for the first-person singular and plural *(let me, let us)*.

> *Let me* go.
> *Let's (let us)* go.

"Third-person" **command**—The **third-person command** is an invitation used for third-person singular and plural *(let him, let her, let it, let them)* .

> *Let it* be.
> *Let them* eat squid.

Note that first and third-person commands use the same construction, "*let...me/them.*"

IN RUSSIAN

The same three types of commands exist, but there is a different construction for each of the three persons. Also, the type of command you are giving will determine the tense and aspect of the verb you choose. Be sure to read the section on aspect in **What is Meant by Tense?**, p. 78, before you read further.

"You" **command**—The **"you"** or **second-person command** is the most common in Russian. It is formed according to rules which vary from one textbook to another. Whatever the rules for formation, the singular familiar *you* command ends in -**ай**, -**и** or -**ь**. The polite plural form adds -**те** to the singular familiar -**айте**, -**ите**, -**ьте**.

■ For general advice, invitations and most negative commands, imperatives are formed from the imperfective aspect.

> *Read and write Russian every day.*
> ⌞general advice⌟
> **Чита́й(те)** и **пиши́(те)** по-ру́сски ка́ждый день.

> *Come in, please.*
> ⌞invitation⌟
> **Входи́(те)**, пожа́луйста.

> *Don't talk nonsense.*
> ⌞negative command⌟
> **Не говори́(те)** глу́пости.

■ For specific commands, including strong negative warnings (about actions that a person might unintentionally perform), imperatives are formed from the perfective aspect.

> *Give me the book.*
> specific command
> **Да́й(те)** мне кни́гу.

> *Call me tomorrow.*
> specific command
> **Позвони́(те)** мне за́втра.

> *Don't forget about the exam.*
> ⌞negative warning⌟
> **Не забу́дь(те)** об экза́мене.

"First-person" **command**—The **first-person** or **inclusive command** *(let us)* is formed by **дава́й(те)** + a conjugated form of the main verb.

■ For general or non-specific commands imperatives are formed by **дава́й(те)** + the imperfective aspect infinitive.

> *Let's read the newspaper every day.*
> ⌞general statement⌟   ⌞repeated action⌟
> **Дава́й(те) чита́ть** газе́ту ка́ждый день.

Let's play.

a non-specific action.
Давáй(те) игрáть.

- For specific commands about complete, momentary actions imperatives are formed by давáй(те) + the future tense from the perfective aspect. The давáй(те) is sometimes omitted, without any loss of meaning.

  Let's sing this song.

  reference is to a specific song
  Давáй(те) споём э́ту пéсню.

  Let's memorize this poem by heart.

  reference is to a specific poem
  Давáй(те) вы́учим э́ти стихи́ наизу́сть.

"Third-person" **command**—The **third-person command** *(let them)* is formed from пусть + the third person, singular or plural, of the present tense, or the future tense from the perfective aspect.

- For general or non-specific commands imperatives are formed by пусть + the present tense. (Remember that the present tense is formed only from imperfective verbs.)

  Let the children sing.

  the action is not limited to a specific action
  Пусть дéти пою́т.

- For specific commands about complete actions imperatives are formed by пусть + the future tense from the perfective aspect.

  Let him sing it himself.

  reference is to a specific "it"
  Пусть он сам э́то споёт.

The following chart summarizes the various forms of the imperative and their Russian equivalents:

	IMPERFECTIVE ASPECT General Advice Invitations	PERFECTIVE ASPECT Specific Commands
2nd person	-ай(те) -и(те) -ь(те)	-ай(те) -и(те) -ь(те)
1st person	давáй(те) + infinitive	давáй(те) + 1st person pl . future tense
3rd person	пусть + 3rd person, sing. or pl. present tense	пусть + 3rd person, sing. or pl. future tense

▼▼▼▼▼▼▼▼▼▼▼▼▼▼▼▼▼REVIEW ▼▼▼▼▼▼▼▼▼▼▼▼▼▼▼▼▼

I. Identify the following imperatives. Are they 1st, 2nd or 3rd person?

1. Let's go away.	1ST	2ND	3RD
2. Go away.	1ST	2ND	3RD
3. Let the children go away.	1ST	2ND	3RD
4. Mark and George, come here.	1ST	2ND	3RD
5. Let us pray.	1ST	2ND	3RD
6. Let them come here.	1ST	2ND	3RD

II. Rewrite the sentences below into commands.

1. We need to exercise more.

_____

2. You should take out the garbage.

_____

3. They should eat clams.

_____

4. We shall not fight.

_____

5. You won't lose.

_____

40. WHAT ARE THE SUBJUNCTIVE AND CONDITIONAL?

IN ENGLISH

The **subjunctive** mood exists in English, but it is used only in a few situations. It occurs in a variety of structures:

1. contrary-to-fact (unreal or implausible) statements

- often introduced by the conjunction *if*

    If I *were* you I *would not interfere*.
    Implication: But I am not you.

    If I *could hand in* the paper on time, I *would be* happy.
    Implication: I will not hand in the paper on time.

- sometimes introduced by a wish

    I wish I *could* write well.
    Implication: I do not write well.

    I wish you *were* dead.
    Implication: You are alive.

2. clauses introduced by certain verbs of asking, demanding, and recommending

    I asked that she *come* to class on time.
    instead of *comes*

    I recommend that he *drop* the course.
    instead of drops

Note that in the subjunctive a third-person singular verb drops the *-s* or *-es* it has in the indicative mood.

Careful

Do not assume that the presence of *would* or *if* automatically indicates the subjunctive. Look at the following examples where these words are used in the indicative mood.

- for an action that has been frequently repeated in the past

    He *would* always *bring* flowers.
    indicative mood

■ to report someone else's words (see p. 155)

He said he *would bring* flowers.
       indicative mood

■ to express the idea of whether or not

I don't know *if* she *is coming*.
       indicative mood

■ to express a condition that is a real possibility

If she *comes* before noon I *will talk* to her.
 indicative mood   indicative mood

IN RUSSIAN

There is no subjunctive mood. Instead Russian uses either the **conditional** mood or the conjunction **чтобы** and a clause (see p. 160) expressing an indirect command. These two constructions express many functions of the English subjunctive.

Conditional Mood

The conditional mood is formed with the particle **бы** + verb in the past tense. Each verb in a conditional statement must be formed in this way. The conditional mood can express contrary-to-fact (unreal or implausible) statements.

> *If you **had given** me money, I **would have** bought a dog.*
> Если **бы** ты **дал** мне де́нег, я **бы купи́ла** соба́ку.
> Implication: You did not give me money. And I did not buy a dog.

> *If you **would work** tomorrow, I **would help** you.*
> Если **бы** ты **рабо́тал** за́втра, я **бы помогла́** тебе́.
> Implication: It is unlikely that you will work. And I will not help you.

> *If only I **knew how to speak** Russian!*
> Если **бы** я то́лько **уме́ла** говори́ть по-ру́сски!
> Implication: I can't speak Russian.

While Russian uses past-tense verbs to form these constructions, the verbs are not past tense in meaning. They acquire tense only from context.

*If you **had worked** yesterday, I **would have helped** you.*
Если **бы** ты **работал** вчера́, Я вы помогла́ тебе́.

*If you **would work** tomorrow, I **would help** you.*
Если **бы** ты **работал** за́втра, Я вы помогла́ тебе́.

Conjunction "чтóбы" + Verb

The conjunction **чтóбы** + verb in the past tense can express a desire for someone else to do something. Translating this type of construction into Russian frequently causes a problem for students because they have difficulty recognizing what is often hidden in the English statement.

Let's look at a typical example of this construction.

I told Peter to buy me a newspaper.

This sentence is made up of two clauses:

> 1. Report clause—"I told Peter..." introduces or "reports" the command.
> 2. Command clause—"...to buy me a newspaper"

This English construction masks how these two clauses are joined. To parallel the Russian construction, rewrite the English sentence joining the two clauses with the conjunction *that*.

I told Peter ***that he should buy*** me a newspaper.

> "...that he should buy..." corresponds to the Russian structure

> "**чтóбы**" + subject + verb in the past tense

Here are some additional examples showing the restructuring of the English statements and the Russian equivalent.

*I told Peter **to buy** me a newspaper.* →
*I told Peter **that** he **should buy** me a newspaper*
Я сказа́ла Петру́, **чтóбы** он **купи́л** мне газе́ту.

*I want you **to read** aloud.* →
*I want **that** you **should read** aloud.*
Я хочу́, **чтóбы** ты **чита́л** вслух.

*The teacher will want us **to take** the test.* →
*The teacher will want **that** we **should take** the test.*
Учи́тель захо́чет, **чтóбы** мы **сдава́ли** экза́мен.

▼▼▼▼▼▼▼▼▼▼▼▼▼▼▼REVIEW ▼▼▼▼▼▼▼▼▼▼▼▼▼▼▼▼▼▼▼

I. Each of the sentences below contains *would* and/or *if* . From the perspective of Russian, circle which sentences express the conditional mood (CM).

1. If Mark gives me the money, I'll buy a car.   CM

2. Mark said he would give me a car.   CM

3. Mark would often give me flowers.   CM

4. If Mark would give me the money, I would buy a car.   CM

5. If Mark hadn't told me, I wouldn't have known.   CM

6. If Mark doesn't tell me, how will I know?   CM

II. Identify the sentences below which contain "masked" indirect commands. Rewrite these sentences to expose and express the command.

1. I told Yura to study more.

_____

2. I want you to come here.

_____

3. She wants her own room.

_____

4. Yura wanted me to call you.

_____

5. Yura told me that she is going to study more.

_____

41. WHAT IS A PARTICIPLE?

A **participle** is a verb form which is part verb and part adjective; when it is used to modify or describe something it is called a **verbal adjective**. Participles have voice (they can be active or passive) and tense (present or past).

IN ENGLISH

There are two participles: present and past. You will have no trouble recognizing them:

The **present participle** is easy to identify because it is the *-ing* form of the verb: *running, working, studying*.

The **past participle** is also easy to identify if you remember that it is the form of the verb you would use following "I have": I have *spoken, written, walked*.

Participles have three functions which are important for students of Russian:

1. The present and past participle may combine with auxiliary verbs to form tenses. Consult the sections on tenses.

> She is *working* today.
> present participle
> present progressive tense

> She has been *working* all day.
> present participle
> present perfect progressive tense

> I have *told* you everything.
> past participle
> present perfect tense

> I was *told* everything.
> past participle
> past tense, passive voice

2. Present and past participles may be used as adjectives; it is principally when they function as verbal adjectives that we identify them as participles.

- attributive adjectives (see p. 61)

Sinyavsky is an *outstanding* writer.
          |
          present participle
          active voice
          modifies *writer*

The *published* article is a well *written* piece.
     | |
     past participle   past participle
     passive voice   passive voice
     modifies article   modifies *piece*

- predicate adjectives (see p. 55)

Brodsky's poetry is *outstanding*.
                    |
                    present participle
                    active voice modifies *poetry*

3. Present and past participles may be used in **participial phrases.** The entire phrase (see p. 159), which does not have a subject of its own, modifies the subject in the main clause (p. 160).

participial phrase
modifies subject *he*

While **reading** *his book,* he drank a cup of tea.
       |
       present participle
       active voice

participial phrase
modifies subject

Filled *with curiosity*, I finally asked a question.
|
past participle
passive voice

IN RUSSIAN

There are two very different types of participles, the **adjectival participle** often called a **verbal adjective** and the **adverbial participle** often called a **verbal adverb.** Unlike English participles, these do not combine with auxiliary verbs to form tenses.

The Verbal Adjective

The verbal adjective corresponds to the function of English attributive and predicate adjectives (see 2 above). It has four forms: present, active and passive, and past, active and passive. The endings will help you to identify most, but not all of these forms. Consult your textbook to learn the rules governing their formation.

Present active participle → formed from imperfective verbs + -щий in the masculine singular nominative

> **рабо́тающий** челове́к
> *a working man*

Present passive participle → formed from imperfective verbs + -мый in the masculine singular nominative.

> **люби́мый** друг
> *a beloved friend*

Past active participle → formed from imperfective and perfective verbs + -вший or -ший in the masculine singular nominative.

> челове́к, **написа́вший** э́ту кни́гу,...
> *the person who wrote this book,...*

Past passive participle → formed from perfective verbs + -нный or -тый in the masculine singular nominative.

> **прочи́танный** текст
> *the text which was read* (or *the read text*)

All four participles can function as attributive adjectives (see p. 61), but only past passive participles can be used as predicate adjectives. Let us look at the rules governing participles used in these two functions.

- Attributive adjectives (present active, present passive and past active participles)

  As adjectives they agree with the noun they modify, i.e., they reflect the noun's gender, number and case.

  > *I know the woman **reading** that book.*
  > Я зна́ю же́нщину, **чита́ющую** э́ту кни́гу.

  | fem. sing. noun accusative case | present active participle modifies **же́нщину** the direct object |

*We spoke about our **beloved (favorite)** professor.*
Мы говори́ли о на́шем **люби́мом** профе́ссоре.

present passive participle   masc. sing. noun
modifies **профе́ссоре**   prepositional case
the object of the preposition **о**

*I want to talk about the problem **solved** by you.*
Я хочу́ говори́ть о **решённой** ва́ми зада́че.

past passive participle   fem. sing. noun
modifies **зада́че**   prepositional case
object of the preposition **о**

- Predicate adjectives (past passive participle)

  Short-form past passive participles function as predicate adjectives. They agree with the noun they modify, i.e., the subject, in gender and number. (Don't forget that short-form past passive participles do not decline and that all genders have the same plural form .)

  *When **was** this letter **written**?*
  Когда́ э́то письмо́ **бы́ло напи́сано?**

  neut. sing. noun   short-form past passive participle
  modifies **письмо́**

  бы́ло shows past tense

  *These houses **will be built** soon.*
  Э́ти дома́ ско́ро **бу́дут постро́ены.**

  pl. noun   short-form past passive participle
  modifies **дома́**

  бу́дут shows future tense

  You will find additional examples of short-form passive participles used as predicate adjectives on p. 142.

Verbal Adverbs Used in a Participial Phrase

The verbal adverb corresponds to the function of the English participle in participial phrases (see 3 above).

Listed below are the two forms (present and past) of verbal adverbs. Consult your textbook to learn the rules governing their formation. As adverbs, they are invariable, i.e., they do not change form to show gender, number or case. The phrase in which the verbal adverb appears does not have a subject of its own; it modifies the subject in the main clause.

Present or imperfective verbal adverb → formed from imperfective verbs.

It is used when the action in the participial phrase is going on at the same time as the action of the verb in the main clause:

these actions occur at the same time

While *reading* the newspaper, he fell asleep.
Читáя газéту, он заснýл.

present verbal adverb **читáя**
in participial phrase
modifies subject **он**

these actions occur af the same time

*Not **knowing** what to say, Masha kept silent.*
Не **знáя** что сказáть, Мáша молчáла.

present verbal adverb **знáя**
in participial phrase
modifies subject **Мáша**

Past or perfective verbal adverb → formed from perfective verbs. It is used when the action in the participial phrase is completed before the action of the verb in the main clause begins.

action A is completed   before action B begins

Having read the newspaper, he fell asleep.
Прочитáв газéту, он заснýл.

past verbal adverb **прочитáв**
in participial phrase
modifies subject **он**

action A is completed   before action B begins

Having passed our exams, we shall go to Moscow.
Сдав экзáмены, мы поéдем в Москвý.

past verbal adverb **сдав**
in participial phrase
modifies subject **мы**

The chart below summarizes Russian participles.

ADJECTIVAL PARTICIPLES (VERBAL ADJECTIVES)		
Attributive They agree with noun modified in gender, number and case.	1. present active imperfective aspect)	рабóтающий человéк a *working* man
	2. present passive (imperfective aspect)	любúмая кнúга a *favorite* book
	3. past active (imperfective and perfective aspect)	дáма, чытáвшая кнúгу a lady, who was *reading* a book студéнт, сдáвший экзáмен a student *who had passed* an exam
	4. past passive (perfective aspect)	прочúтанное письмó a *read* letter (*which has been read*)
Predicate They agree with noun in gender and number.	1. past passive (perfective aspect) short-form	Письмó прочúтано. The letter *is read.* Всё бýдет сдéлано. Everything *will be done.*
ADVERBIAL PARTICIPLES (VERBAL ADVERBS) —for participles in participial phrases		
They are invariable.	1. present (imperfective aspect) action simultaneous to action in main clause	Читáя письмó, он заснýл. *Reading* the letter, he fell asleep. Не вúдя дрýга, он ушёл. Not *seeing* his friend, he left.
	2. past (perfective aspect) action comes before action in main clause	Кóнчив рабóту, он ушёл. *Having finished* his work, he left. Позáвтракав, я ушлá. *Having finished breakfast,* I left.

Careful

Not all words that end in -*ing* are participles in English. Furthermore, not all participles which end in -*ing* are translated into Russian with a participial form. Study the sentences below which summarize the various English -*ing* words and their Russian equivalents .

1. present participle in progressive tense (see p. 82) → various tenses, no participles

> Masha *is working* and Ivan *will be working*.
> present progressive   future progressive
> Máша **рабóтает** и Ивáн **бýдет рабóтать**.
> present
>   future (imperfective aspect)

2. present participle as adjective → present active participle

> A *smoking* volcano is dangerous.
> verbal adjective, modifies *volcano*
> **Куря́щийся** вулкáн опáсен.

3. present participle in participial phrase → present adverbial participle (verbal adverb)

> *Laughing* loudly, she left the room.
> verbal adjective in a participial phrase
> Грóмко **смея́сь,** онá вы́шла из кóмнаты.
> verbal adverb in a participial phrase

4. gerund → infinitive

> *Smoking* is harmful to your health.
> gerund
> **Курúть**—здорóвью вредúть.
> infinitive

▼▼▼▼▼▼▼▼▼▼▼▼▼▼▼▼REVIEW ▼▼▼▼▼▼▼▼▼▼▼▼▼▼▼▼▼▼▼

Identify in each of the sentences below the function of the participle which is in *italics*. Is it used to form: a verb tense (VT), a verbal adjective (VA), or a participial phrase (PP)?

1. She was *reading*.	VT	VA	PP
2. The woman *reading* is my aunt.	VT	VA	PP
3. While *reading*, the woman felt ill.	VT	VA	PP
4. Is this ham already *smoked*?	VT	VA	PP
5. I gave her a *smoked* ham.	VT	VA	PP
6. When she had *smoked* her cigarette, she left.	VT	VA	PP
7. A *smoking* cigarette caused the fire.	VT	VA	PP
8. Had you been *smoking*?	VT	VA	PP
9. *Smoking* constantly, he paced the room.	VT	VA	PP
10. *Annoyed* by the noise, I left.	VT	VA	PP

42. WHAT IS A GERUND?

A **gerund** is a word which is part verb and part noun; it is sometimes called a **verbal noun**.

IN ENGLISH

The verbal noun or gerund is formed with the dictionary form of the verb + -*ing*. It looks like, but does not behave like, the present participle (see **What is a Participle?**, p. 145).

The verbal noun can function in a sentence in almost any way that a noun can: as a subject or as the object of a verb or of a preposition. Look at the different functions of the verbal noun *smoking* (from the verb *to smoke*) in the three sentences below:

Smoking is harmful to your health.
subject

Do you enjoy *smoking?*
direct object

What do you think about *smoking?*
object of the preposition

IN RUSSIAN

There is no gerund or verbal noun in Russian. The gerund is most often translated by an infinitive.

Smoking *is harmful to your health.*
gerund
Кури́ть—здоро́вью вреди́ть.
infinitive

*I enjoy **swimming**.*
gerund
Я люблю **пла́вать.**
infinitive

The gerund also may be translated by a noun. For instance, the Russian noun for "singing" (**пение**) is like a gerund in that it is derived from a verb, but unlike a gerund in that it is not freely formed from any verb and is not called by a special name in Russian.

> *I like her **singing**.*
> |
>   gerund
>
> Её **пение** мне нра́вится.
> |
> noun

Careful

Words ending in *-ing* in English have many different functions; it is very important that you be able to distinguish them in order to choose the correct Russian equivalent. Study the sentences on p. 151 which summarize the various *-ing* forms in English and their Russian equivalents.

43. WHAT IS DIRECT AND INDIRECT SPEECH?

We can divide speech into **direct speech** , that is, speech which we place in quotation marks to show that we are quoting directly someone's words, and **indirect** or **reported speech**, that is, speech which repeats or reports, but does not quote, someone else's words.

Read the following conversation in which three people are participating:

direct speech	**A**: "I *am coming*."
	B: "What did he say?"
reported speech	**C**:"He said that he *was coming*."

Observe that when C repeats, but does not quote, what A has said, he changes the verb *am coming* to *was coming*. The change of verb tense in C's report of what A said is called **sequence of tenses** in reported speech.

IN ENGLISH

In changing direct speech into reported speech, the speaker must make the following changes:

1. PRONOUN—make any necessary changes in the pronoun.

2. TENSE—change the tense of the "reported" verb to make clear that the action of the verb took place at an earlier time.

Look at the ways that English changes tense from direct speech to reported speech:

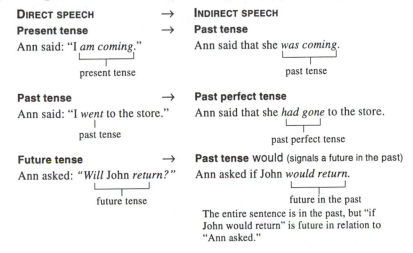

DIRECT SPEECH	→	**INDIRECT SPEECH**
Present tense	→	**Past tense**

Ann said: "I *am coming*."   Ann said that she *was coming*.

present tense   past tense

Past tense	→	**Past perfect tense**

Ann said: "I *went* to the store."   Ann said that she *had gone* to the store.

past tense   past perfect tense

Future tense	→	**Past tense** would (signals a future in the past)

Ann asked: *"Will John return?"*   Ann asked if John *would return*.

future tense   future in the past

The entire sentence is in the past, but "if John would return" is future in relation to "Ann asked."

IN RUSSIAN

The tense of the verb used in a reported statement is the same as it would be in quoted or direct speech, i.e., there is no sequence of tenses.

You must be able to do the following:

1. IDENTIFICATION—Recognize indirect speech.

2. TENSE—Change the tense of the verb in indirect speech so that it is the same as it would have been in direct speech.

> *She said that she **was reading**.*
> <u>past tense</u>
>
> 1. IDENTIFICATION: *to say* often introduces indirect speech.
> 2. TENSE: Change *was reading* to present tense *is reading*.
>   (Direct speech: She said: "*I am reading.*")
>
> *She said that she **is reading**.*
> Она́ сказа́ла, что **чита́ет**.
> present tense

> *Ann said that he **would return**.*
> <u>past tense *would*</u>
>
> 1. IDENTIFICATION: *to say* often introduces indirect speech.
> 2. TENSE: Change past tense *would return* (a past-tense view of future time) to future tense *will return*.
>   (Direct speech: Ann said: "*He will return.*")
>
> *Ann said that he **will return**.*
> Анна сказа́ла, что он **вернётся.**
> future tense

▼▼▼▼▼▼▼▼▼▼▼▼▼▼▼REVIEW ▼▼▼▼▼▼▼▼▼▼▼▼▼▼▼▼▼▼

I. Rewrite the sentences below from reported speech into quoted speech.

1. John said he would be late.

_____

2. When did Mary say she would go to the store?

_____

3. Vika told me that she had bought a house.

_____

II. Rewrite the sentences below into reported speech following the rules of sequence of tenses.

1. Ivan wondered, "Will she marry me?"

_____

2. I asked, "Did Mark take his test?"

_____

3. Ann asked, "Are you coming to my house?"

_____

III. From the perspective of Russian, which has no sequence of tenses, rewrite the sentences below so that the verb tense in reported speech will be the same as it needs to be in Russian.

1. He said that he was busy.

_____

2. She asked if you would come.

_____

3. Katya asked if we were coming to her house.

_____

44. WHAT ARE SENTENCES, PHRASES AND CLAUSES?

What is a Sentence?

A **sentence** is the expression of a complete thought; it will usually
contain at least a subject (see **What is a Subject?**, p. 19) and a verb
(see **What is a Verb?**, p. 68).

Raskolnikov confessed.
   subject   verb

Depending on the verb, a sentence may also have direct and indirect
objects (see **What are Objects?**, p. 24).

The woman gave Raskolnikov the money.
 subject verb indirect   direct object

In addition a sentence may include various kinds of modifiers: adjectives (see **What is an Adjective?**, p. 60), adverbs (see **What is an
Adverb?**, p. 99), prepositional phrases (see **What is a Preposition?**,
p. 93) and participial phrases (see **What is a Participle?**, p. 145).

The *old* woman gave Raskolnikov the money.
 adjective
modifies *woman*

Finally the old woman gave Raskolnikov the money.
adverb of time
answers the question *when?*

Finally the old woman gave Raskolnikov the money
in spite of her fears.
   prepositional phrase

Finally, *persuaded by the young student's poverty*, the old woman
               participial phrase
               modifies *woman*
gave Raskolnikov the money in spite of her fears.

What is a Phrase?

A **phrase** is a group of two or more words expressing a thought, but without a subject or a conjugated verb.

with a smile
armed with a smile
to disarm your enemy with a smile

We identify phrases by the type of word that introduces them.

- **prepositional phrase** → begins with a preposition

through the door
| |
preposition   object of preposition

after the concert
| |
preposition   object of preposition

- **participial phrase** → begins with a participle

leaving the room
| |
present   object of *leaving*
participle

pasted on the wall
| |
past   prepositional phrase used
participle   adverbially to modify *pasted*
of *to leave*

- **infinitive phrase** → begins with an infinitive

to learn Russian
|__| |
infinitive   object of *to learn*

to read intelligently
|__| |
infinitive   adverb modifying *to read*

To recognize such phrases you need to find the individual parts (prepositions, participles, infinitives) and notice how the group of words works as one block of meaning.

What is a Clause?

A **clause** is a group of words containing a subject and a conjugated verb. It forms part of a compound or complex sentence. There are two kinds of clauses: main (or independent) and subordinate (or dependent).

A **main clause** expresses a complete thought, the essential idea of the sentence. If it stood alone with a capitalized first word and a period at the end, it could be a simple sentence. It is called a main clause only when it is part of a larger sentence.

complete sentence

Raskolnikov knew.
subject   verb

main clause

Raskolnikov knew that the old woman had money.
subject   verb

A **subordinate clause** cannot stand alone as a complete sentence. It must always be combined with a main clause.

main clause   subordinate clause

Raskolnikov knew that Sonia loved him.
subject   verb   subject   verb

Sentences which contain a main clause and a subordinate clause are called **complex sentences.**

▼▼▼▼▼▼▼▼▼▼▼▼▼▼▼REVIEW ▼▼▼▼▼▼▼▼▼▼▼▼▼▼▼▼▼

Underline any dependent clauses you find in the sentences below.

1. If I were you, I would be patient.
2. I don't know when he will get better.
3. Without Emily's help, we can't finish the work.
4. We did take a walk, even though it was raining.
5. By the time we arrived, the fight was over.
6. We shall leave tomorrow after your breakfast.

ANSWER KEY

1. **What is a Noun?** 1. Jones, tour, seashore 2. Moscow, capital, Russia, city, culture 3. Reading → a gerund or a verbal noun (see p. 153), pastime, subways 4. patience, virtue 5. Russians, Pushkin, father, heritage 6. students, diligence, perseverance 7. Soviet Union, rate, alcoholism 8. price, food, salary

2. **What is Meant by Gender?** 1. M 2. F 3. ? 4. N 5. N 6. F 7. N 8. M 9. ? 10. M

3. **What is Meant by Number?** I. 1. dress 2. loaf 3. family 4. tooth 5. woman II. 1. ы 2. и 3. я 4. и 5. ы 6. и 7. а 8. а

6. **What is a Subject?** 1. Q: What rang? The bell. Q: Who ran out? The children. 2. Q: Who took the order? One waiter. Q: Who brought the food? Another (waiter). 3. Q: Who voted? The first-year students (or The students.) 4. Q: What assumes? That. Q: Who is right? I. 5. Q: What is difficult? It. Q: What is a beautiful language? Russian.

7. **What is the Possessive?** (the possessor is in *italics*) 1. the meow of the *cat* 2. the cost of the *books* 3. the husband of my older *sister* 4. the letter of *Nina* 5. the second child of *Peter*

8. **What are Objects?** (indirect objects are in *italics*) 1. cake, *mother* 2. kiss, *mama* 3. flowers, *Vika* 4. tea 5. kiss, *me*

9. **What is a Predicate?** (predicate adjectives are in *italics*) 1. *kind* 2. doctor 3. *busy* 4. professor 5. *younger, older*

10. **What is a Pronoun?** (the antecedent, if stated, is in *italics*) 1. you → *Mary;* she → *Ann* 2. itself → *book;* nobody; it → *book* 3. what; this; it → *fudge;* herself → *Mary* 4. anyone; which → *book;* he → *Mark* 5. which → *route* 6. I; I; yours → *pen*

11. **What is a Personal Pronoun?** I. 1. I, я 2. she, она́ 3. they, они́ 4. you, ты 5. we, мы 6. he, он 7. you, вы 8. it, оно́ II. 1. вы 2. мы 3. они́ 4. вы 5. ты 6. вы 7. они́ III. 1. оно́ 2. он 3. она́ 4. они́ 5. они́

12. **What is a Possessive Pronoun?** (possessive adjectives are in *italics*) I. 1. *my*, yours 2. *your,* ours 3. *her,* hers 4. mine, his 5. *my, your* II. 1. his 2. my/ mine 3. our/ours 4. her/hers 5. their/theirs 6. your/yours (formal and plural) 7. your/yours (familiar singular)

13. What is a Demonstrative Pronoun? (demonstrative adjectives are in *italics*) 1. *this*, *that* 2. *this*, that 3. that 4. that, *these*, those 5. *these* 6. those

14. What is an Interrogative Pronoun? (interrogative adjectives are in *italics*) I. 1. what, *whose* 2. *whose*, whom 3. *what*, who 4. *which*, what (the second "which" is a relative pronoun) II. 1. who? 2. what? 3. who? what? which? which one? 4. whose 5. what? which? what kind of? III. 1. what 2. what 3. what

16. What is a Descriptive Adjective? (predicate adjectives are in *italics*) 1. young → woman, *sad* → woman 2. younger → students, *eager* → students 3. tired → I, morning → run 4. international → flights, *late* → flights

23. What are Transitive and Intransitive Verbs? (direct objects are in *italics*) 1. v.t., *Russian* 2. v.i. 3. v.i 4. v.t., *child* 5 v.t, *books* 6. v.i. 7. v.t., *friends*

26. What is the Present Tense? I. 1. reads 2. is reading 3. does read II. 1.present 2. past 3. present 4. past 5. past

27. What is the Past Tense? I. 1. I wrote, I was writing, I had written, I had been writing, I did write 2. she swam, she was swimming, she had swum, she had been swimmming, she did swim II. 1. imperfective 2. perfective 3. imperfective 4. imperfective 5. imperfective 6. perfective 7. imperfective 8. perfective

28. What is the Future Tense? I. 1. I shall read, I shall be reading, I shall have read, I shall have been reading 2. she will cook, she will be cooking, she will have cooked, she will have been cooking II. 1. imperfective 2. imperfective 3. imperfective 4. perfective 5. perfective 6. imperfective 7. perfective

29. What is a Preposition? I. 1. at, by 2. without 3. before, in, by 4. due to, beyond, instead of II. 1. For what are you going to the store? 2. I don't know about what are you talking? 3. Between whom is the fight? 4. In favor of whom did you vote?

30. What is an Adverb? I. 1. carefully → drives 2. too → difficult 3. well → speaks 4. everywhere → rides 5. very → well; well → behaved II. (the adjectives are in *italics*) 1. nicely 2. *nice* 3. fast 4. *fast* 5. *sudden* 6. suddenly 7. late 8. *late*

31. What is a Conjunction? 1. P 2. C 3. P 4. C 5. C

32. What is a Relative Pronoun? I. 1. This is the car that/ which I plan to buy. 2. I saw the film that/ which you liked. 3. The car that/ which I like is too expensive. II. (relative clauses are in italics) 1. Who was that masked man *to whom you were talking?* 2. What's the name of the restaurant *about which you're always talking?* 3. Where's the new teacher *with whom I saw you?* III. (1. *that* is a conjunction 2. *that* is a demonstrative adjective) 3. that 4. who (5. *who* is an interrogative pronoun 6. *which* is an interrogative adjective) 7. which (8. *that* is a conjunction) 9. that (10. *that* is a demonstrative adjective) IV. (the antcedent is in *italics*) 1. that, *letter* → DO 2. who, *woman* → S 3. whom, *man* → OP 4. which, *desk* → OP

33. What is a Reflexive Pronoun? 1. myself 2. yourself/yourselves 3. ourselves 4. herself 5. yourself 6. himself

34. What is an Intensive Pronoun? 1. RP, yourselves → you 2. IP, yourself → you 3. IP, himself → director 4. IP, herself → director 5. RP, yourself → Lena 6. IP, himself → Vanya 7. IP, themselves → they 8. RP, ourselves → we 9. RP, yourself implied *you* (2nd person imperative) 10. IP, yourself → you

35. What are Indefinite and Negative Pronouns and Adverbs? I. 1. never 2. no one 3. nothing 4. nobody 5. nothing 6. nowhere 7. nowhere II. 1. never, anyone, anywhere → I have *never* seen *no one nowhere* with such a long nose. 2. nobody, anything, anybody → *Nobody* said *nothing* about *nobody.* 3. never, anywhere → I *never* go *nowhere* alone.

36. What is Meant by Comparison of Adjectives? I. 1. boring (P) 2. most energetic (S) 3. better (C) 4. best (S) 5. less convincing (C) 6. busiest (S) 7. busy (P) II. 1. cheaper (AA) 2. taller (PA) 3. more popular (AA) 4. shorter (PA) 5. shorter (AA) 6. cheaper (PA)

37. What is meant by Active and Passive Voice? I. 1. I returned the books. 2. The Spartak team won the game. 3. Your friend wrote the letter. II. 1. The book was written by me. 2. Will the lawn be mowed/mown by you? 3. Free tickets were given to them by the producer. III. 1. P 2. A 3. P 4. A 5. A 6. P

39. What is the Imperative? I. 1. 1st 2. 2nd 3. 3rd 4. 2nd 5. 1st 6. 3rd II. 1. Let's exercise more. 2. Take out the garbage. 3. Let them eat clams. 4. Let's not fight. 5. Don't lose.

40. What are the Subjunctive and Conditional? I. 4. CM 5.CM
II. 1. I told Yura *that he should study more*. 2. I want *that you should come here*. 4. Yura wanted *that I should call you*.

41. What is a Participle? I. 1. VT 2. VA 3. PP 4. VA 5. VA 6. VT
7. VA 8. VT 9. PP 10. PP

43. What is Direct and Indirect Speech? I. 1. John said, "I will be late." 2. When did Mary say, "I will go to the store?" 3. Vika told me, "I have bought a house." II. 1. Ivan wondered if she would marry him. 2. I asked if Mark had taken his test. 3. Ann asked if we were coming to her house. III. 1. He said that he is busy.
2. She asked if you will come. 3. Katya asked if we are coming to her house.

44. What are Sentences, Phrases and Clauses? 1. if I were you
2. when he will get better (3. none) 4. even though it was raining
5. by the time we arrived (6. none)

INDEX